Karl König's Path into A

Karl König's Path into Anthroposophy

Reflections from his Diaries

Peter Selg

Floris Books

Karl König Archive, Vol 2
Subject: Karl König's Biography

Karl König's collected works are issued by
the Karl König Archive, Aberdeen
in co-operation with the Ita Wegman Institute
for Basic Research into Anthroposophy, Arlesheim

Translated by Irene Czech

First published in German in 2006 under the title
Karl König und die Anthroposophie by Verlag am Goetheanum
First published in English by Floris Books in 2008

© 2006 Verlag am Goetheanum, Switzerland
English version © 2008 Floris Books, Edinburgh
Karl König texts © Trustees of the Karl König Archive

British Library CIP Data available

ISBN 978-086315-629-8

Printed in Great Britain
by Athenaeum Press, Gateshead

Dedicated to
the memory of
Peter Roth
(1914–97)

Contents

I told him about my affinity for people with special needs and my question as to whether working with them could be my vocation. He invited me to work in the Camphill movement and recommended that I study Kaspar Hauser's life and Rudolf Steiner's writings about the Fifth Gospel.

Erhard Fucke[1]

That *Anthroposophia* wishes to share and enlighten the destiny of Christianity: this conviction was the main foundation and aim of [Karl König's] life.

Peter Roth[2]

Introduction

For all the inner and outer drama of his life, which enabled him to become a citizen of the world, König was essentially a devout man in a renewed, modern sense made possible through anthroposophy.

Hans Müller-Wiedemann[3]

The aim of this book is to bring to light deeper aspects of Karl König's spiritual life and inner path, thus complementing and extending Hans Müller-Wiedemann's comprehensive biography. The present attempt primarily draws on Karl König's own words — the words he wrote daily in a personal yet supra-personal way to describe the path taken in both inner and outer endeavours, in spiritual research and studies, and finally in establishing the 'Camphill Way'. Beginning already in his youth, Karl König wrote his diaries meticulously and without interruption. These diaries fulfilled a typical 'need for written, historical documentation' (Hans Müller-Wiedemann[4]). While König's diary entries are existential in character, they are never of a 'private-personal' nature. König himself regarded the diary contents as an account of his spiritual life and work — which, of necessity, included his struggles with inner and outer obstacles. In certain respects Karl König 'objectified' his activities through this process of documentation and regarded it as an absolutely essential part of his life and fulfilled it with characteristic determination.[5]

Most of Karl König's diaries do not exist anymore, the majority having been burned in 1987 at the request of Anke Weihs, one of his closest and most trusted colleagues. Only miscellaneous notes from his youth in Vienna, from the periods spent at Pilgramshain and Camphill, as well as the original diaries from 1943, 1944, 1953, and 1955 remain today and are housed in the Camphill Archive at Aberdeen, Scotland. Thanks to the initiative of Margit Engel the extensive typescripts of excerpts from a further eight diaries (1945, 1954, 1956, 1957, 1962, 1963, 1964 and 1966) could be completed before the original material was destroyed. Using these documents as a basis and focusing particularly on the period 1943 to 1966, as well as being prompted by specific quotations in Hans Müller-Wiedemann's biography, already some time ago I began to work on annotated, thematically-organized presentations of Karl König's diary entries, the fruits of which will be published during the course of the coming years.[6]

This study provides a first glimpse into Karl König's inner world and the spiritual development of his work, thus bringing his deep spirituality and humanity to light in a very special way which I hope will be of benefit not least to the current Camphill movement. This short manuscript of selected quotations does not encompass a comprehensive portrait of Karl König,[7] and because of the fragmentary nature of the available documents König's spiritual development cannot be shown. In my opinion, however, this work allows us to meet him directly through his words and to see some of his innermost intentions. It also has the possibility to open the way to the great individuality who continues to be effective, and also to the spirit he served and still serves 'In willing the good / In recognizing the truth, / In loving the Christ.'[8]

This study was written at New Year 2005/6 following a lecture at the Camphill School Community at Forenbühl and within the more specific context of studies on Rudolf Steiner and the Fifth

Gospel[9] 66 years after Karl König and his friends at Kirkton House deepened their work on this subject (New Year 1939/40) in preparation for the move to Camphill House, in June 1940.

The present work is intended to be an inner dialogue with Hans Müller-Wiedemann's core biographical work.

In the years to come, further studies relating to the life of Karl König will appear within the collected works. This work is being done by the Karl König Archive, Aberdeen in co-operation with the Ita Wegman Institute for Basic Research into Anthroposophy, Arlesheim, Switzerland.

Peter Selg
Ita Wegman Institut
Epiphany 2006

1

The Struggle for Existence

Deep dejection still weighs on my soul. I feel completely
alone and abandoned.   *(May 19, 1954)*

If we are honest and we look — not into the silent mirror
— but into the 'speaking eyes' of others and we imagine
how they see us, then I believe not one of us could honestly say: I resemble the human archetype. Because personal destiny and personal suffering have taken hold of us
more and more; they have set the chisel of existence to
work on us, not only forming — but also deforming us.
                                        Karl König, 1964[1]

Karl König struggled with loneliness and melancholia all his life.
He went through recurrent phases of severely depressive moods
and he repeatedly had to summon up all of his courage and will-
power to overcome the obstacles presented by destiny. That is to
say, he had to endure his condition and, moreover, affirm it as a
necessary part of his earthly path. ('The separation and exclusion
from the spirit is as if complete. Sometimes have the impression
that my true I is not here at all and I live as an automaton, merely
responding to emerging and fading memories.' (Oct 2, 1957.)
König also struggled with his physical constitution,[2] the burden
of a choleric temperament and his impatience, as well as with
countless experiences of 'not belonging' and the consequent
sense of isolation, 'Experience myself as a stranger amongst people' (April 20, 1954). König did, in fact, frequently experience

being 'the outcast', also in outward events. As a Jewish refugee he narrowly escaped persecution by the Nazis; when three sisters and one of his father's brothers died in the concentration camps he lost the supportive foundation of family for his life in Central Europe.[3] König was excluded from the General Anthroposophical Society in 1935; this followed intensive debate and inner struggle on his part, but also after attacks on his character and misjudgments regarding his chosen path that soon arose after his first public appearances within anthroposophical circles. König came to the anthroposophical movement as a solitary individual and an outsider, with burning social concerns and questions. His powerful presence, however, already evident in the early lectures and essays asked too much of the established anthroposophical context and its capacities for 'integration'.[4] Nevertheless, König's ever-renewing path of suffering had a karmic imprint and stood in relation to a higher, Michaelically-inspired battle for the light in dark times and for the appearance and receiving of the coming Christ-Sun through processes of suffering and transformation.[5]

Karl König's diaries and notes offer a compelling testimonial of his all-encompassing struggle through daily life burdened further by recurrent periods of illness. The diary entries are evidence of König's merciless honesty with himself and with respect to the errant ways of body, soul environment which he unceasingly tried to overcome with spiritual counterforces and will-power, although in the process he often experienced himself as a failure. His notes of July 26, 1954, a Saturday evening, provide a typical example of this:

> It was a bad night again and in the morning the irritation
> is so great that I am filled with anger and accusations.
> Cannot do my exercises, cannot pray and I am filled with
> a kind cynicism that I have never experienced before.
> Feel like the spirit has beaten me, and rather than being
> grateful, I rebel and shut myself away with false pride

and foolish indignation. ... But then I am very exhausted and must go to bed again and so cannot take part in the Bible Evening. Alix is also not going to go, and so it was a day full of defiance and resistance, and it is a disgrace that I could not resist any of it.

In another diary entry from this period, one characterized by recurrent illness, he writes:

It is a dark and gloomy day, dominated by headaches and feeling ill. The tiring cold continues and my forehead is so heavy that inner work continues to be futile. My soul is silent and dull — as if all forces of love have passed away and been lost. I cannot overcome the inner discontent, and doubt and darkness prevail. (Jan 12, 1954)

There were many occasions when, after many hours of effort and spiritual work, Karl König managed to overcome the inner crises that frequently afflicted him at the beginning of the day. On December 29, 1957 he wrote:

Am free of headaches in the morning but during meditation it begins again with such intensity that my bad mood and anger rise up from inside like an unconquerable power. Cannot tolerate people around me and shut myself away, in shame.

Am I being tested, now, during the Holy Nights — and am I failing these tests?

During the afternoon I struggle with the material for the evening lecture. Read various passages by Rudolf Steiner concerning the form taken by the archangels, and their activity, and only gradually a fuller picture begins to develop. I must make an effort to overcome the morning outburst by evening, but dark flames continue to smoulder. The lecture develops in a free and beautiful

---

Wednesday May 25

Die Nacht war halbwegs gut sob-
wohl ich wenig schlafe, bin ich am Morgen
recht ausgeruht. Nach der Morgenme-
ditation aber beginnt wieder ein stark
negativer Gefühls- > Gedankeninhalt
in mir sich breit zu machen. So daß ich
hoffnungslos > zynisch werde + nichts
mehr gelten lassen will. Dann aber
lese ich einen, an sich gar nicht so
wichtigen, Artikel von Prof. I. Wach über
„Das Selbstverständnis des modernen
Menschen" + als er darin von der Imma-
nenz des religiösen Gegenwart zwischen
Gott + Mensch spricht, fallen Schuppen von
meinem Herzen + es beginnt sich etwas
zu regen, was ich gegen Abend aufschrei-
ben kann. Es beginnt mit den Worten:
„Alles mögest Du wissen"! + versucht
die Notwendigkeit darzustellen, daß
die Geistes-Wissenschaft allein, nicht
helfen kann, sondern das unmittelbare
Erleben Gottes das Notwendige ist. Fühle
mich tief schuldig in meinen Verfehlungen.

Diary entry of May 25, 1955. See page 81 for translation.

way, however, and only then do the smoke clouds finally disappear. Afterwards am deeply grateful that I was able to survive it all.

Karl König suffered immense disappointments in the social sphere time and again, and experienced himself — and Camphill — also in later years, as repeatedly excluded, ignored and undervalued. At the same time he constantly reflected on feelings that arose out of a situation, but were nevertheless rooted in his own soul tendencies — feelings that he persistently struggled with but was never able to completely transform:

> The night was dull and inactive, and my head is still shrouded in darkness and shadow. In the morning I briefly read the news of the South African Anthroposophical Society in the morning; irritation wells up in me and I feel hurt and deceived. But I know that this is utterly wrong, and that I have no authority at all over the South African work. I struggle the entire day with these emotions, the bane of my life; it is a kind of envy and a desire to possess, and I know that I must become more humble if I am to outgrow this transgression.
>
> Signed many letters in the evening and then went to bed very tired. Will I win the battle? (Feb 6, 1962)

In contrast, the following entry of June 10, 1955:

> During the past days I have continually made the effort to overcome the discontent that has kept me so occupied. Discontent and anger about Arlesheim, the teachers, Dornach ..., just everything that I experience as opposition, over and over again. And I do not know how I can free myself from all these negative feelings and thoughts. They bore into me like an evil worm, all the time. But then, the light dawned in the morning in such a way that I could see that all of them, exactly as myself,

had to carry the burden of an earthly destiny, and that
they had to — willingly or unwillingly — play their
roles. This gave me the freedom to be able to love them
again — to love without demand.

★

At the same time, however, it would be erroneous to regard
Karl König's soul struggles — which he documented compre-
hensively, thus willingly and consciously leaving behind this
testimonial for his contemporaries and for future generations
— merely as an expression of his destiny-bound constitution,
that is, of his own individual earthly struggle, or to interpret
these solely as a necessary stage along his path of inner schooling. Although partially infused with trauma and characterized
by temperamental outbursts — and as such, partly also a
process of transforming karma — König's suffering and the
criticism brought against him also reveal objectively identifi-
able deficits in the development of civilization and in the
Anthroposophical Society — deficits which König perceived
with as much sensitivity as wakefulness. In this way, the com-
bination of his extraordinary sensitivity and his 'lack of
belonging' in life had the character of a 'sensing instrument'
borne out of pain which led him to recurring crises through
its particularly activity. At the same time, however, this 'instrument' should not, in its spiritual sense, be underestimated as a
Christological organ of conscience. 'The pain and shame
about the behaviour of the anthroposophists welled up
strongly in me again. It is a wound that cannot be healed.'
(June 7, 1956). The development and realization of the
Camphill movement in a spiritual sense was inseparably
bound up with König's perseverance and productive transformation of his experiences of social deficit and was, at least partially, an answer to these.[6]

2

The Inner Path

The structure of my inner life only transforms during the exercises.

(July 1, 1956)

In the morning the Foundation Stone Meditation is extremely penetrating and I experience that the Michael Imagination should replace the fourth verse; only then can the Foundation Stone become for Michaelmas what it is for Christmas.

(Sep 29, 1957)

At the request of Camphill co-workers, Karl König held lectures about the schooling path of spiritual science from January 1953. When these lectures were taken up again on February 4, 1960 at Newton Dee, König introduced the subject in the following way:

I must honestly confess that I have always cast [this subject] to one side because I knew — and still know — that one cannot speak deeply enough about these things. I would go even further and say that it is simply impossible to give a lecture when the true meaning of the subject being presented can only be discovered by way of inner silence. If I go on to speak now in spite of this restriction, no-one should expect me to give a lecture in the usual sense. Perhaps together we can try to listen to the spaces between the words.

What should we speak about? Rudolf Steiner gave a number of indications. He took us by the hand, as it were, and he still guides us on the inner path if we want to follow him. No doubt we often fail to take his advice, to pay attention to his recommendations or to read exactly what he has suggested. However, what we can do together — and that is all that I can offer you — is to remind ourselves of certain important indications that he gave.[1]

Although Karl König wanted to limit his lectures to reviewing Rudolf Steiner's descriptions of the schooling path of spiritual science, his presentations nevertheless revealed the depth of experience out of which he spoke. Already during the founding phase of Camphill, he had accompanied and supported individual co-workers on a safe meditative, esoteric path — clearly a path he had systematically pursued since the beginning of the 1920s. As the Newton Dee lectures and also his diary indicates, Karl König sought direct connection with Rudolf Steiner's statements — indeed with Steiner himself — for orientation and guidance along the path. 'He still leads us on the inner path if we want to follow him.'[2] Therefore König returned again and again to Rudolf Steiner's texts and specific formulations: On July 1, 1956 he remarks:

During the past weeks I studied the first hundred pages of *Knowledge of Higher Worlds* with more insight than previously, and it seemed that only now the indications could become real for me.

The structure of my inner life only transforms during the exercises. Thinking can be better grasped and therefore it can be directed. And the world of dreams also becomes a little livelier. But above all, I clearly realize how far behind I am with all inner exercises. It is good that this is understood.

While Karl König did not write or leave behind any notes concerning his inner meditative practice, many diary entries document remarkable experiences of the inner space of awakening in the morning. As such, these experiences belong to the specific moment of crossing the threshold back into the earthly world. König had immense spiritual gifts and he clearly schooled his consciousness systematically and with finely differentiated spiritual organs, for the 'moment of awakening' and the sphere within which it takes place. With respect to making progress along a spiritual schooling path and therefore also intensifying awareness of night experiences, Rudolf Steiner repeatedly emphasized the necessity for very fine perception of the 'moment of waking' and active involvement in it, 'that the outer world is not conjured all at once before the soul, but that the soul, without as yet regarding the outer world, feels itself surrendered to what has been experienced within.'[3] In the pre-Easter period of 1955, on March 9, Karl König noted the following:

> I always wake up at 5 AM and then in the growing
> morning light it is possible receive important insights
> which arise and then also pass away, becoming
> submerged. This time I may be closer to the M.o.G.
> [Mystery of Golgotha]: We should always carry the
> image of the Crucified One in our soul so that we may
> escape the deeds of the thieves on the cross; we should
> see ourselves in this way — with arms and legs bound —
> so that gradually we will lose all aggression.

Two weeks later, in the days between March 21 and 25, König wrote about experiences at the threshold of awakening — experiences that were concerned with existence in the 'Spirit of Ocean-Being'. On March 21, he writes:

Wake up at 3 AM; there is a very bad south-easterly storm outside, rattling the windows as if it wants to smash them. Must try to withstand this because it relentlessly wants to overpower me. I am tossed back and forth together with my self like a boat on a wild sea until I begin to realize that my thinking is light, and in this way I can experience it as a peace-bringing force. But in this moment the spiritual world appears before me like an ocean of light and a voice invites me to sail out onto the waters; fear overwhelms me and I speak inwardly, 'I will only go when the Christ calls me!' In this moment silence descends within, and the storm suddenly abates. Peace surrounds me. The day is uneventful. Tired from the night and what has been experienced, I can hardly do anything. Make the effort not to lose what has been experienced.

Two days later he writes:

Am awake early again, about 5 AM. And once more I am able to experience the spiritual world as an ocean — but in darkness, and I see myself walking on a beach; something like C.D. Friedrich's painting of *The Monk at the Sea*. I know now that we are only able to build the boat in that we practice thinking; then there are boards; the harmonized feelings, however, are the sails with which the spirit-wind can weave itself. A completely new experience awakens, one that has not been accessible before.

On March 25, in a third account, König records the following:

Once again a short night. Wake up very early; the beach and ocean of the spirit gradually open up before me again. I connect this with inner experiences of the Class

Lessons and it seems to me in our day and age there is an unrelenting fear of experiencing this land. It is the ocean upon which the resurrected Christ walks.

★

Further entries describing the beginning moments of König's day — the world of experience surrounding his morning meditative exercises — show that the spiritual-scientific content he brought in his lectures and writings as well as the specific impulses for the development of Camphill were drawn in original form from this spiritual space. Thus on November 6, 1944 his brief notes read:

> While meditating [in the morning] experienced many essential things for the Community; wrote these down. Also saw the etheric form of three animals: cow, lion and eagle.

Some of these experiences came about through the morning awakening process described above and König would then develop and contemplate these meditatively. Thirteen years later, on November 29, 1957 he wrote again with respect to Camphill and the community's spirituality:

> While half-asleep something touches me and it seems as if the 'Angel of Buddha' were shown to me, and how the community would be guided by this spirit. Do not understand this at all. Only when I wake up properly and am able to remember, waves of gratitude wash through my soul — because this is Colchis and the Golden Fleece, and Iphigenia and the great Buddha Mysteries. All before me, like a great, unfinished painting that can still be sensed, and I experience the grace in this encounter.

Ideas and insights concerning themes that König had studied into the night also often came to him during his regular morning meditations:

> In the morning meditation found the connection between the sense organs and the insect groups. Attempt to develop this and achieve a degree of success during the day. (Jan 17, 1944).

> Early on during meditation sensed the position and function of the pineal gland; wrote about it at length (April 18, 1944).

> During morning meditation the full power of electricity and magnetism become visible to me. The effect of these elements underlying the Earth's existence and the basic structure of their fields in the human being; here the masculine and feminine are revealed and provide profoundly meaningful insights. Try to think this over and also to follow it up. (March 14, 1953).

> In the morning, during meditation, I suddenly have a picture showing me that all music instruments originate from metamorphosis of the bird's body. See this in the violin structure which is little more than a transformed bird form. Now I know why birds sing and what music vibrations really are. (Aug 5, 1957).

On July 12, 1945, only two months after the end of the Second World War his notes read:

> During meditation in the morning, step into the landscape of the dead. Experienced this as the world of the ethers and marvel at its similarity to our own surrounding world. Now I know why people travel.

Many of Karl König's morning awakening experiences concerned his own destiny. As Rudolf Steiner had described in

Wednesday February 4

Am Morgen beim Aufwachen, als ich den Vorhang vorziehe, erlebe ich etwas mir Wesentliches: Daß das Auge gar nicht dazu da ist, die Dinge + Gegenstände zu sehen, sondern dazu, um den Raum zu bereiten, in welchem die Dinge + Gegenstände „sich sehen lassen können". Denn ich erlebte, wie das Licht mich durch draup durch das Auge hindurch + dadurch ich Anteil nahm an einem Lichtraum, der sich um mich herum ausbreitete. Dadurch, daß das Auge diesen Raum erzeugt, wie eine Kerze, die in der Dunkelheit angezündet wird, erscheinen die Dinge innerhalb dieses Raumes + bezwingen mich sie wahrzu- nehmen.

Dann sah ich die Raphael-Kartons + besonders den wunderbar-lebendigen über „Hüte meine Schafe".

Am Nachmittag Kinder + obwohl sehr interessant, mit wenig innerer Anteil- nahme + Erleuchtung.

Diary entry of February 4, 1953. See page 81 for translation.

various lectures, during the night — the sphere of sleep — the human being confronts and recapitulates to a certain extent his eternal individuality's previous incarnations. 'The whole karmic past ... passes before the human being every time he sleeps.'⁴ So that the tasks of the current life on earth can be taken up each morning with fortified strength and focus. At Breslau, on June 14, 1924, Rudolf Steiner said that indications of the karmic dimension of individual existence could be discovered by means of very fine observation. 'The moment of waking brings a faint indication of what an individual bears within him from his past earthly lives.'⁵

Karl König saw himself as frequently confronted with huge obstacles in his earthly life with which he had to struggle for long periods. He found direction for the course of his life and destiny journey through questions and searching. During a journey to Vienna, in the pre-Christmas period of 1954, shortly before the onset of a serious heart complaint and confronted with the city of his birth, he wrote the following in his daily review with regard to the moment of awakening in the morning:

> This morning I know with great certainty that it was right that I was born a Jew. Until now my search for the meaning of this has been fruitless. But now I understand that during childhood and teenage years I was again able to immerse myself in the Hebraic-Jewish element, and was therefore able to assimilate — right to the bone — the witnessing of the Mystery of Golgotha. (Dec 13, 1954)⁶

Numerous further notes show how intensively König's morning awakening experiences were connected to the destinies of the Thirty Years' War and with Wallenstein.⁷ Thus he had noted on October 14, 1944: 'Wake up in the morning with an impression of Paracelsus' death. Know that he was reborn as Wallenstein. 24.IX.1541 [Paracelsus' death] / 24.IX.1583 [Wallenstein's birth]. This is how destiny works and a child happens to be there.' More than ten years later, during severe attacks of cardiac angina which had begun soon after his journey to Vienna, this experience unexpectedly surfaced again.

> I wake up at 4 AM but there is no seizure. The stabbing in my heart aches and is painful, and then I instantly know that it is the same stabbing carried out by the senior butler; the whole problem opens up and I am able to recognize the karma; but have the strength to leave it open and not become fixed about it. But the Thirty Years' War is once again so close, as if it had happened yesterday. (Feb 9, 1955)

Two weeks later this experience is amplified once more and further background is revealed to Karl König. He records this as follows:

> A strange night. Wake up at 3 am, without pain but with great anxiety. Powerful experience of Wallenstein's death and how he did not take on the battle against the three beasts, consequently bringing about his fall through the outer deed of murder. The burning of Jakob von Molay emerges from the background of this death, as if Paris, Prague and Vienna would hold out helping hands to each other. Must try to be firm and steadfast with the emergence of the beasts and the abyss. It all lasts until about 5 AM. Then I can sleep again. (Feb 24, 1955)

The illness that König died of eleven years later was ultimately to affect the heart — the centre of human life, the primary organ of conscience, destiny, transformation and the activity of the Christ.[8]

3

Spiritual Work

I wake up very early in the morning (it is about 4 AM) and
begin to think about the lecture on 'The Cosmic Word'. A
few ideas come to me, but nothing decisive happens. I get
out of bed and sit down to do my preparation. And then it
begins to flow and it is as if everything forms itself.

(Aug 5, 1962)

An essential not to be underestimated part of Karl König's spiritual work was his lecturing activity on the widest variety of subjects: Christology and the history of thinking and ideas; biographies and historical events; the seasons and cosmology; social questions; anthropology and biology; medicine and curative education and many more areas of human life and civilization. Karl König himself decided on many of these themes as a result of perceiving, recognizing or sensing their relevance at a particular point in time. Other lecture themes arose in response to requests or questions either from inside or outside the community. The scope and breadth of content, the detailed elaboration and particular spiritual quality of his lecturing work is quite exceptional and was not achieved by any other pupil or colleague of Rudolf Steiner in this productive way. König's diary entries show the extent to which he lived into the content of his lectures, and show the extraordinarily dynamic — at times breathtaking — process of preparation, and its culmination often only a few hours before the beginning of a lecture.[1] König immersed himself in these events with total spiritual openness and sincerity. In this sense his lectures were not a first communication of insights that had already been worked on and developed but rather an account of a current event. In spite of his extensive knowledge and intensive occupation over years and decades with certain subjects and motifs, his lectures still essentially concerned experiences of the present and immediate past, and incorporated their particular and unique source. Karl König wrote the following on April 10, 1965, the day before his Palm Sunday lecture about 'Cosmic-Breathing and Cosmic-Pulse' at Föhrenbühl, 'Tomorrow's lecture has announced itself: Cosmic breathing and cosmic pulse. What does this want to become?'

In the same entry, König wrote the following observations about the development of his work during the course of the day:

> Step by step — I stay in bed in the morning — human breath and human pulse become visible; also how the breath undermines the pulse and thus destroys the spirit seed, which is, of course, identical to the phantom. Here are the beginnings of a new Christian anthropology.
>
> Prepare myself during the afternoon and increasingly the theme reveals itself and shows me its many different facets. It is remarkable to participate in this process of unveiling. Nevertheless difficult to find the right words and expressions.[2]

Listeners who were sceptical and critical of Karl König dismissed many of his presentations and repeatedly accused him of fantastic embellishments and excesses, if not pseudo-imaginative suggestion. However, König's diaries show how self-critical he was, not only of his lectures but also with respect to many of his inner experiences that were not shared with others blindly but rather worked through from different perspectives.[3] It is not possible to deny that König often spoke very quickly — occasionally also too quickly[4] — about his most recently attained insights, that he demanded too much from many of his listeners with his imaginative or imagination-like style,[5] and did not always succeed in explicitly presenting an adequate level of insight. The diaries, however, enable at least an initial understanding of how existential certain subjects and lecture commitments were for König — in other words, the level of spiritual courage and trust in the spiritual world involved in 'enlivening' his preparation.[6] Not least, with regard to anniversaries of deaths and biographical events, König was obviously acting out of consciousness of a higher task. In a certain sense he grew into this task, serving it selflessly and engaging in it with the greatest possible will.

On August 17, 1954 he noted: 'In the evening I begin to read books by Schelling so that I will be prepared for the hundredth anniversary of his death day.' The following day he writes, 'In the morning I have the impression that I should try to organize a commemorative evening for Schelling on Friday so that the friends here can become aware of this great individual.' One day later he continues:

> Today is a complete rest day for me; stay in bed and read a lot about and by Schelling. Gradually an image of him forms in my soul and I am particularly absorbed with his deep connection to Caroline. Who was Schelling? He did not belong to the circle of the apostles, like Novalis and the two Schlegels and others, yet he must have been very close to them. Is Nicodemus in the background? One can experience something thoroughly Magdalena-like in Caroline, but who wants to know this?
>
> It is wonderful, to be able to be immersed in this whole epoch, with its magic and greatness, and to be close to those who had such an immense impact on it. I begin to understand, or better, to sense how Herzeloid-Tycho inspired him.

Finally, with regard to Schelling's death day, König noted the following on August 20, 1954:

Wednesday May 18

Heute ist Gustav Mahlers Todestag;
vom Morgen an bin ich irgendwo dorthin
ausgerichtet. Vor 44 Jahren starb er,
noch recht jung; doch ein Vollendeter.
Lese in Alma's Buch über seinen Tod;
suche die schöne Photographie heraus,
die ich von ihm habe. Abends höre ich
dann mit Alix zusammen die 2. Symphonie; es ist schön; rührend, dieses
Meisterwerk wieder zu erleben. Dann
erinnere ich den Traum, den ich einst
hatte, nachdem ich sein Grab besuchte;
nun wird mir offenbar, wie diese 2.
Symphonie nichts anderes darstellt, als
die Auferweckung des Lazarus. Ja, das
ist es; vielleicht war Mahler dabei ge-
wesen; hat es dann wieder - erahnt.

Sonst ist nicht viel Wesentliches. Sehe
Norvenna, die mir lang von Cairulee
erzählt. Auch lese ich eine sehr wichtige
Arbeit von Prof. Haubold über Rouge-
lismus, die gerade erschienen ist.

Diary entry of May 18, 1955. See page 81 for translation.

Read ... the lecture by Rudolf Steiner where he speaks about Fichte, Schelling and Hegel, drawing a link between the loftiness of their idealistic imaginations and the spirituality of Krishna. And I have to consider that Krishna is the Nathan Jesus and therefore his spirit sun illumines the three of them. Thus it would have been his individuality which reigned in the Michael School of the last century, and it was Tycho de Brahe who held up the mirror to receive the rays of this Sun, and thus inspired Schelling.

The evening will turn out well. Veronika Bay will sing Wolf and Schubert songs at the beginning and end, and I will speak at length about Schelling and read small excerpts from *Weltaltern, Bruno* and the *Philosophy of Revelation*.

★

During the course of the most immediate lecture preparation, the period of intense concentration and wrestling with spiritual questions around a particular subject, König's efforts would often bear fruit with the help of one of Rudolf Steiner's lectures that he frequently stumbled upon quite unexpectedly. That is, breakthroughs were achieved on pre-imaginative, imaginative, inspiration or intuition levels of knowledge, indicating the further course that his research and studies should take. His diary entry of January 4, 1962, is typical of such an event, written in the context of his preparation for a music therapy conference at Camphill.

The mystery of bird song is taken up again on the basis of one of Rudolf Steiner's lectures, and during the study of the bird skeleton it suddenly becomes clear that the bird's body is a larynx; the breast bone, the thyroid cartilage, the shoulder blade, the cricoid cartilage etc., but the neck and beak are similarly windpipes, tongue

33

and mouth, and in this way the whole bird is a producer of sound. This discovery fills me with joy. But it will not be understood when I present it at our course.

During preparation Karl König would work intensively with Rudolf Steiner's lectures and books which he had come to know through repeated readings, and would formulate specific questions in relation to the current theme. Quite clearly, König was repeatedly able to access the spiritual depths out of which Rudolf Steiner had once spoken to his listeners. In one process of 'spiritual disclosure' which König had striven for with deliberate intention and the greatest possible strength, it unexpectedly occurred 'out of itself' so to speak. ('And then it was revealed to me ...') He was clearly overwhelmed as his notes of Sunday, May 1, 1955 show.

> During the night am again awake a long time; then tired in the morning. I make a great effort when reading the eighth lecture of *From Jesus to Christ,* particularly with the passages where Rudolf Steiner speaks about the Nathan spirit. There it is gradually revealed to me, and it is as if the scales fell away from my eyes. He is Christian Rosenkreutz. This completely transparent ego, devoid of sin and carried by the Christ for three years, became the apostle who received the special initiation in the thirteenth century. The crucified Christ: he is Christian Rosenkreutz. Now a number of things begin to appear in a completely new light.

★

During his lectures, König often experienced deeper dimensions of the content with which he had created a vital connection during the course of his intensive preparation, and it was *out* of this living content he actually experienced himself speaking. He wrote the following with regard to his description of the

Saturday February 21

Vormittags versuche ich, mich auf
die nun bevorstehenden Vorträge, besonders
den ersten, über: „A new approach to
Sense-Perception" vorzubereiten. Es wird
schwer eine richtige „Er" leuchtung zu
bekommen & so stopple ich einiges von
dem zusammen, was ich sowieso weiß &
mache eine Art Vortrag daraus & fühle
mich sehr beschämt.

Es sind dann viele Menschen da & ich
beginne zu sprechen & der Geist wird beginnt
zu wehen; aber in der Mitte des Vortrags
wird es still um mich & nur mit Mühe setze
ich die Worte aneinander & empfinde eine
grenzenlose Leere. Sehe mich selbst von außen,
zappeln wie ein Fisch am Sand. Kann dann
doch fertig sprechen.

Der zweite Vortrag über „Riechen & Schmecken"
wird viel besser. Er ist durchweht & ich bin
selber erstaunt wie lebendig & geistesfüllt ich
sprechen darf. Das Erlebnis der Gnade & der
Dankbarkeit dafür ist groß.

Abends spricht Michael Wilson. Nachher bin
ich so müde, daß ich am Bibel-Abend nicht
mehr teilnehmen kann.

Diary entry of February 21, 1953. See page 81 for translation.

'Cosmic Lord's Prayer' and its link to the Foundation Meditation within the context of his lectures of January 1954, towards
the end of the Holy Nights.

> Prepare myself for the evening lecture. Work very
> precisely on the connection between the Cosmic Lord's
> Prayer and the Foundation Stone Meditation and repeat
> the events of the laying of the Foundation Stone for
> myself so that I can describe it accurately.
>
> Initially very difficult because the voice does not yet
> want to speak, but gradually it becomes possible and
> during the description of the scene where Jesus
> collapses at the pagan altar, it is revealed to me that the
> voice of the Bath-Kol is the voice of the Christ himself
> which sounded through the larynx of the Nathanic
> spirit. The lecture turns out well and is impressive.
> (Jan 4, 1954)

He then notes the following with regard to the lecture given
on the following day, January 5:

> Speak ... in-depth about the structure of the Foundation
> Stone Meditation and its nine parts, and their connection
> with the nine lines of the Cosmic Lord's Prayer. Towards
> the end of the lecture I am so overwhelmed that I can
> hardly speak, and I know: It is the Christ who spoke the
> words of the Foundation Stone Meditation through the
> mouth of Rudolf Steiner.

In such moments Karl König saw himself in the service of the
spiritual world, its spiritual beings and intentions — in contrast to
the many occasions where he clearly considered his lectures as
unsuccessful. These events were, for him, gifts of mercy and he
experienced them almost soberly and without personal vanity. He
respected these processes as an expression of the fact that the
earthly efforts to understand supersensory content about hierarchical beings can be particularly perceived, observed and fostered

when they stand under a sign of gratitude and deep reverence for the world of the dead. Rudolf Steiner himself repeatedly made such references which König, for his part, incorporated as a guiding principle of his inner life and spiritual work, and indeed, also within the Camphill culture.[7] König wrote the following in retrospect with regard to a lecture given in Stockholm on February 20, 1954 after a day of too many appointments and overexertion.

> Then the many children who must be examined, and conversations, and all this goes on until 5 o'clock in the afternoon. Am completely exhausted and drained as I sit down to prepare for the public lecture. As if in the very last moment, the key thoughts are given to me, and they are the characteristics of the three beasts: Haste in thinking, emptiness in feeling, laziness in the will. The concert hall is full and I begin with a trumpet blast: 'The social question is a human question, and the human question is a question of education'. It becomes a great lecture, very powerful, and at the end, I feel myself entirely as an instrument of Chr. R. [Christian Rosenkreutz].

★

Finally, eight years later, König made notes regarding even more deeply penetrating — and for him, profoundly moving — lecture experiences in Spring Valley, USA during the course of numerous presentations he had developed about human speech and movement. On July 25, 1962 he noted:

> In the morning must prepare in the shortest possible time for the second lecture about 'speech'. In connection with what was described the day before yesterday there are completely new insights regarding the threefold speech process and the second Fall of Man at the

building of the Tower of Babel. Am overwhelmed by this. During the lecture I feel a minor attack of faintness wanting to overwhelm me, but am able to resist it. Then it is possible to present everything, and it is as if I am filled with the spiritual substance that was once active at Ephesus.

Four days later, on July 29, König continued:

Wake up very early and prepare myself for the lectures in thoughts and pictures. Speech appears to be the origin of all the arts. Yes, walking, speaking and thinking and the highest of the senses are the totality of the seven arts, as Rudolf Steiner once presented them. Eurythmy, however, is not 'another' art form, but a renewal of all the arts.

For König the entire preparation and lecturing process at Spring Valley culminated at the end of the first week of August with an intensity that he had not experienced previously. On August 5 and 6, he wrote:

Wake up very early in the morning (it is about 4 AM) and begin to think about the lecture on 'The Cosmic Word'. A few ideas come, but nothing decisive happens. Get out of bed, sit down to prepare. Then it begins to flow and it is as if everything forms itself. In the process of formulating the conclusion — and because I understand that the Cosmic Word sounds from the planets and that the 'World-Creator-Being' expresses it — I know that Rudolf Steiner is present and is present in me. I am moved to tears and then I begin the lecture; but it is Rudolf Steiner himself who gives the lecture. At the end, a wave of shock runs through the audience. I can hardly keep my composure.[8]

Am still completely dazed in the morning. But a deep love for Rudolf Steiner — as never before — fills my

heart and I try to use what I experienced and learned
yesterday to keep myself awake. I remember that he was
here as if in golden robes, not clothed in black as usual.
Also sense that this week's Soul Calendar verse 'Can I
expand the soul' is relevant to this experience. I spoke
the Cosmic Word itself and this took place through
Rudolf Steiner. Why am I allowed to be an instrument?
Possibly because a significant impact must be made on
the work here in America.

As with the processes of preparation and lecturing, König also
had intense spiritual experiences during the writing of his many
essays and books. Notwithstanding his extensive scientific studies that were either the focus of his work on a particular subject
or running parallel to it, the writing of an essay or a book was, for
him, a wholly creative process. Through the struggle to find a
suitable language — that is, the Logos-spirituality appropriate
for the phenomenon that was to be described — König penetrated ever deeper layers of a subject's potential content. 'Am
amazed how everything develops out of the writing itself'
(March 10, 1944). In this sense, he never wrote down what was
complete and fixed in its final form. Also here he experienced a
process that could only be partially grasped in the beginning and
of whose development and fruition he was an integral part. On
July 23, 1954 he gives a typical account.

The day is used almost exclusively for writing. An
essay emerges about the acquisition of the faculty of
'walking' in the first year of life, and after the first
sentence is written down, after some effort and strain,
I am able to continue to write smoothly and to
describe how learning to walk is a kind of birth process
that proceeds from the head downwards. How directed
movement is born step-by-step out of the undirected
movement and how yet another occurrence is linked to

this: The child separates its body-consciousness from
its experience of the environment, and is thus able to
sense a distinction between self and world. That,
however, becomes the basis for further mental
development.

Three days later he writes:

This evening it was possible to finish writing the essay
about 'walking'. First I try to describe 'hereditary
movement' and to provide evidence of its relationship to
symptoms in paralysed children (athetosis, spasticity,
disturbances in postural and static reflexes). In the
process it becomes clear how the different forms of
paralysis are nothing other than forms of movement that
have not been mastered in early childhood. Then I also
try to explain the 'calendar' of the brain within the circle
of the year, and thereby the image of the shepherd
(walking) amongst the herd (hereditary movement)
arises. Without having to say it, learning to walk appears
as grace conferred on the child by the Christ.

At the end I am able to put down my pen, filled with
gratitude. (July 26, 1954).

On February 15, 1955 — following long periods of illness —
König writes another entry in his diary in this regard:

Afterwards I am able to write the first paragraph about
speech. And while writing, speech presents itself as a
spirit and tries to speak. This is very strange to me, and
magical — in the sense of Novalis.

Many comparable — in themselves extraordinary and
impressive accounts — can be found in Karl König's diaries
about the progress and development of his inner search for
knowledge and insight which unfolded during the writing
process. König's writing activity concerning individual studies of

Rudolf Steiner's *Soul Calendar* took place over a long period of time, and in reference to this, he noted the following at intervals over many years:

> Continue to write in the Soul Calendar book in the afternoon and work with the four Light verses (fifth week). Suddenly it is revealed that a system of circulating light interacts between Nature and the human soul during the course of the year. (May 19, 1955).

> Continue writing the Soul Calendar essay. Realize that the word 'spirit-depths' indicates world ether and human ether and is connected to light circulation.
> (May 2, 1965).

> Have the whole day ahead of me and hope to write another part of the essay that was started yesterday. ... The work progresses rapidly because the sequence of the first verses (No. 2, 3 and 6) and their opposites carry 'loss' and 'discovery' like an open secret within themselves. Am struck again by the word-architecture of these verses which flow from Rudolf Steiner's intentions in every respect. It is as if the cosmic Word is speaking here. I make a fair bit of headway during the day with new and rather wonderful results. (Jan 20, 1966).

In contrast, König was able to produce other written works within a few days or weeks. Parallel to his many different Camphill tasks and duties he dedicated himself to writing with immense concentration and devotion and was often completely captivated and fascinated by what came to meet him spiritually. In the second half of May 1954, König wrote the following remarks about the steps taken in the development of his great essay on sepia.[9]

> Really bad sinus infection starts in the morning. My head hurts miserably and thinking is impossible. Deep

Wednesday December 9

Kann wieder schreiben & setze dort fort,
wo ich vorige Woche aufhören musste. Versuche
die Darstellung der drei Räume, des Sehraums,
Tastraums & Hörraums; leite aus einer Ver-
schiebung dieser Räume zueinander, das Phä-
nomen des Schwindels ab. Auch wird jetzt die
Struktur des Schädels noch durchsichtiger, damit
die Zuordnung von Schädelhöhle, Vestibular-
Apparat, Augenmuskeln, zu den drei Räumen.
Damit ergibt sich die dreifache Struktur des
Gleichgewichts-Sinnes. Im Schädel ist er Kopf,
im Bogengang-System ist er rhytmische Organisation & in den Augenmuskeln ist er Glied-
maßen organisation.

Arbeite dann für mich, ohne es darzustellen aus, wie im Auge die Beine, besonders der Oberschenkel, sich metamorphosiert
& in der Mittelohr-Bildung die Arme sich
strukturell wiederholen.

Diese Arbeit wächst über mich hinaus & ich
muss vorsichtig sein, nicht davon überwältigt
zu werden.

Diary entry of December 9, 1953. See page 81 for translation.

bitterness wells up and I cannot control it. Feel punished by the spiritual world but do not know why and for what. Then in the afternoon I try to concern myself with the sepia medicine so that the promised essay can be written. My wretched head prevents the breakthrough and I am unable to grasp the archetypal image of molluscs and the octopus. (May 15, 1954).

Wake up in the morning with even worse pain and am in a state of bitterness and negativity the entire day. Every single thing shows its evil and bad side and I despair deeply. I doubt Camphill and myself, and repeated attempts to find an explanation of the image of sepia all end in confusion. An agonizing predicament. (May 16, 1954).

Deep dejection still weighs on my soul. Experience myself as completely alone and abandoned and am under the impression that the spiritual world has cast me out. (May 19, 1954).

Am able to continue writing, and now the path leads in such a way that it is possible to recognize that all cephalopods appeared directly after the Moon's emergence — therefore, in the middle of the Lemurian epoch — and so the place of sepia substance in the course of Earth evolution becomes clear to me. This also reveals the place of melanin as a skin pigment in contrast to that of iron-blood pigment. (May 24, 1954).

Send my apologies to School's council, and am therefore able to finish writing the sepia essay in the afternoon and evening.

Everything that could be correlated from the anatomy, physiology, behaviour and origins of the octopus pinpoints characteristics that can be easily and clearly classified. Am happy about this because it is the first time I have been able to formulate such a clear image of a

medicinal substance on a spiritual scientific basis.
(May 26, 1954).

Rewrite some pages for the sepia paper in the morning
and correct the remaining sections. Am not very satisfied
with what has been produced because it is like a not-
quite-structured piece of work, and more like an
energetic initial step that does not quite achieve what was
required. Nevertheless decide to send it and include a
letter to Gisbert Husemann explaining this.
(May 31, 1954).

After a long period of time Karl König finally received the gal-
ley proofs of the sepia essay. Surprised and pleased he wrote the
following in his diary:

Read the print-outs of the sepia essay written a year ago
and now to be published in the *Beiträge*. Am astonished
how much is accurate and true in this essay ...
(July 28, 1955).

★

The way in which König researched relevant themes and motifs
during the days and weeks of a writing project — and how the
final written work was a kind of 'answer' to this process — can
be further understood through many of his biographical studies.
An example may be found in König's notes of Spring 1956
before he began to write about Sigmund Freud's life and work, a
theme he had already taken up and studied a number of times.
König noted on March 15, 1956 that he had recently occupied
himself again with Sigmund Freud's biography, 'I am also con-
tinuing to read about Sigmund Freud's life and it is very moving
to see the mystery character of it all more and more clearly,
although in a state of decay.' Two days later he decided to give
priority to writing a study on Freud.

> In the morning suddenly sense a voice that urges me not
> to continue writing the essay about the meaning of the
> word and thought. 'That work is for Easter time.' So I
> put it aside and focus entirely on Freud. Begin to read a
> great deal about his life and now know the title of the
> paper: 'The destiny of Dr Sigmund Freud'. A number of
> things become clear in the process, particularly
> concerning the close connection to [Josef] Breuer, in
> turn to Rudolf Steiner, then to Wilhelm Fliess and
> thereby to [Hermann] Swoboda and [Otto] Weininger.
> All this belongs to the essential destiny of this person.

Four days later, on March 21, 1956 he again wrote in this
regard:

> In the afternoon read much about Freud and this
> personality fascinates me increasingly. The entanglements
> of destiny become more and more strange, and gradually
> he appears as an opponent of Rudolf Steiner. A genius
> without any true humour. Full of pride, sarcasm and
> filled with powerful emotions, but like an inactive
> volcano that could erupt at any moment. Negatively
> critical and entirely Jewish. Will I retain enough
> objectivity to be able to write something about him?

A day later, König had to travel to Belfast via Glasgow where
he was expected by Carlo Pietzner on March 23 at Camphill
Glencraig. On the eve of his departure he remarked in his
diary:

> Storming and raining heavily. Not at all inviting for
> travel and a journey. As the essay about Freud is just
> about to be born, I ask myself if the trip should be
> cancelled after all. Then conscience speaks strongly,
> urging and advising me to make the journey, so I cast all
> my lethargy aside.

Sunday September 20

Am Morgen beginne ich dann zu schreiben
s bringe es ein wenig vorwärts. Dann lese ich
ich Kolisko's Aufsatz über Druidens Barden s
da ahne ich, warum er auf dem Bahnhof
Paddington sterben mußte. Von dort gehen
die Züge nach Westen, nach Wales s nach
Tintagel, nach Glastonbury s Penmaenmawr.
Und nun kann ich schreiben s das erzählen,
was mir wichtig erscheint aus diesem
seltsamen Leben.

Jetzt wird auch ersichtig, warum er sich
in Wien inkarniert hat; er ging dorthin,
wo eine musikalische Sphäre ihn umgeben
konnte, so daß sein musisch-bardisches
Wesen nicht zu einsam in dieser modernen
Umwelt sich fühlen mußte.

Als ich am späten Abend fertig geschrieben
habe, bin ich befriedigt. Ich weiß wieder, wie
eng ich mit diesem Schicksal verbunden bin
s das gibt einigen Trost in der vorhandenen
Not s Seelenleere.

Um 7³⁰ starb im Krankenhaus der
Kleine Andrew Paton, der als letztes
Masern-Kind der Epidemie vor einigen
Tagen nach Aberdeen gebracht wurde.

Diary entry of September 20, 1953. See page 81 for translation.

Am cold on the way to the station and the journey to Glasgow is thoroughly uncomfortable. Surrounded by rain, mist and storms, it is more like November than pre-Easter. Continue to read at length about Freud and discover, for example, that he attended a number of philosophy semesters with Franz von Brentano, and so his opposition to Rudolf Steiner becomes clearer.

König continued this work while on the ship to Belfast, but was temporarily interrupted because of consultations with the children at Glencraig and other activities, including the first reading of a Class Lesson* in Ireland ('Now, for the first time, the Class has come to Ireland, and thus the Irish Cross has been added to the Rose Cross.' March 25, 1956). Nevertheless König persistently revisited his writing project and the relevant reading material. On March 27, the evening of his return journey, he noted:

Although the crossing is peaceful, only sleep a little bit and continue to read at length about Freud. Feel even more strongly obsessed with the subject and decide to take on the task of writing an essay over Easter so that I can finally free myself of it.

König actually began to write a few days later and continued during Easter. On Easter Sunday he wrote:

Continue to work on the Freud essay. The encounter with Fliess, and consequently also with Weininger, and then more about Freud's character and behaviour. Describe him as an Orpheus searching for his Eurydice; Orpheus, who, in the process of his descent, forgot who he was searching for. He lost himself in agnosticism in the same way.

---

* The First Class (of the School of Spiritual Science) is a course of lessons on spiritual development including a sequence of meditative verses, open to members of the Anthroposophical Society on application.

The following day, Easter Monday, he noted:

> Make further effort on the Freud essay and try to show
> how, at the highpoint of his insights, what he describes
> as Eros and Tanatos was a clear representation of the
> realms of Lucifer and Ahriman. But the third, the Christ
> standing at the centre, is missing. Thus his last book
> about Moses becomes a denial of Christianity.

On April 3 Karl König completed the essay. In a certain sense
the tragic content had affected him deeply during the entire day
but at the same time he recognized the necessity for the work.
'Afterwards I write a section of the essay about Freud. His inabil-
ity to recognize Christianity and his consequent decline through
isolation and loneliness.'[10]

★

Finally, König's Mystery Plays, written between 1941 and 1962,
are amongst his great written works and also bear the characteristics of the way he lived and worked — with inwardness and
creative receptivity to the spirit.[11] Various surviving diaries show
the inner situations which inspired his writing and how, step by
step, the work was then accomplished. When reviewing the day
on Whit Sunday, June 4, 1954, König wrote the following about
the possibility of a Whitsun play and the beginning development
of its concept:

> Have breakfast with Tilla and the children in the
> morning but there is little feeling of Whitsun. Later,
> during the children's service — I am able to be there —
> something infinitely delicate takes place, and again I
> sense the presence and lofty visit of the 'Three Kings'.
> But now I know a bit more: Epiphany is the day of the
> Baptism with the Holy Spirit and the Day of the Kings. I
> experience them as the intimate carriers of spiritual

substance, and this where an outline of the Whitsun play falls into place. The setting must be two bridges and so I begin to write in the afternoon. Is this Whitsun?

In June 1962, exactly eight years later, also during the Whitsun period, König's diary notes describe the story of the birth and further development of a new play *(Zarathustra's Chalice)*. The initial impulse towards writing this play came about on June 1, followed attendance of the Emmaus play *(The Evening at Emmaus* which was originally written in 1952):

> Attend the Emmaus play in the evening. Am deeply moved ...
>
> There is a devout quality in the interpretation, and it is now pressing that other plays are written in order to provide a complement to this beginning. I treat this desire with earnestness.

Already on the next day he wrote:

> A very busy day. Two sides to it: Outwardly many conversations; inwardly a new 'play' begins to unfold. I notice it is set in the house of Salome and that the two sons, John and James play definite roles ...
>
> The play emerges in the evening and it is possible to write the first two scenes about Salome, Martha and Thomas.

During the following days, between June 3 and 6, König noted how this work progressed:

> The play continues to develop. Thought at first that the figure of the Risen One himself appears. But with a closer look this is the appearance of the Jesus child who carried the Zarathustra ego until the three-day scene in the temple at Jerusalem. Why this is so, I do not yet understand at all ...

Use the evening to continue writing. The conversation with Thomas develops — his despair, Salome's sceptical superiority. Then the Jesus child appears. But I do not get much further; it is like a darkness is concealing everything. (June 3).

Inside, the child insists and wants to find its place. But I cannot quite understand it. Read through what has already been written so that an even stronger connection can be made. (June 4).

Wake up during the night at about 3 AM and cannot sleep anymore. Now the scene with Salome and the Jesus child progressively takes shape. Get out of bed and write until 6 AM. Am deeply moved by the content and the way in which this comes about, in my presence and within me. Tears flow down my face. (June 5).

Am able to complete the play in the late afternoon and evening. It develops in such a way that Salome's two sons tell her about the appearance of the Risen One in the Cenacle. All three experience the Lord's presence and so the last of the ice in their hearts melts. Will the hearts of the players and audience also melt? (June 6).

On June 6, the same evening, König presented the newly created play to Alix Roth and noted the following a day later:

Read the play to Alix yesterday in the late evening. Both of us were deeply moved by it. Good that it was completed before Whitsun.

4

The Spirituality of Camphill

The Community is within the actively developing
stream of Christianity. It serves Christianity through
anthroposophy ...

(Sep 7, 1944)

In addition to the comprehensive collection of Karl König's
manuscripts and publications concerning the establishment of
the Camphill community and movement documented and
reviewed in-depth from a biographical and historical viewpoint
by Hans Müller-Wiedemann,[1] of diary entries also show König's
continual process of reflection concerning the spiritual task and
social form of Camphill.

König often noted his own opinions that were formulated
during meetings of the inner community, obviously intending to
keep a record in this way. In August and September 1944, four
years after the purchase of Camphill estate, he wrote:

At the meeting, speak about the necessity for us to find
renewed and deeper interest in each other. That becomes
possible in that one may experience the working of the
Holy Spirit. In relation to the 'other', it depends on the
activity of each individual to light a flame within.
(Aug 31, 1944)

> At the meeting I say that the Camphill community does
> not belong to either the anthroposophical movement or
> to the Christian Community. The [Camphill]
> Community is within the actively developing stream of
> Christianity. It serves Christianity through
> anthroposophy ... (Sep 7, 1944)

A number of diary entries, fragmentary in nature, reveal that also in later years König continued using his diaries for questioning and seeking clarification. Amongst the entries of 1955 and 1956 we find the following:

> The Community sacrifices intellectuality in that it
> cultivates the religious impulse in anthroposophy.
> Goetheanum! (Nov 30, 1955)

> We did ... not take the path of the Christmas Conference,
> but rather chose the path of an order. (May 21, 1956)

★

From the very beginning Karl König felt a deep connection to the people who had emigrated [to Scotland] together with him and who had been part of the original resolution in Vienna to build a community serving the child with disabilities and special needs, in the sense of a Michaelic Christianity and in further fulfilment of the central European mission. On November 4, 1943 he noted:

> Journey into the night. Read the second Mystery Drama
> at length and am deeply impressed. Great ideas for
> Camphill come up and Thomas [Weihs] is particularly
> close to me. Am deeply touched by this.

Karl König clearly regarded the group of people working together at Kirkton House and later at the Camphill estate as a 'mystery community' in the sense of a future Christianity — a community of people closely connected to each other spiritually with a specific, future-orientated work objective. Although the founding group's goals originated wholly in the sphere of freedom and future social culture, at the same time König was conscious that many old karmic connections and conditions were working in the group — active connections between individual participants that created a functional basis for communal tasks and activities. Very early on Karl König recognized his bond of destiny with Tilla Maasberg who became his wife in 1928.[2] She was essential to the unfolding of his entire destiny path from Arlesheim to Silesia and later on, to Camphill, and she created the soul-spiritual substance out of which he lived and worked for the remainder of his life. König also recognized destiny paths with other community members, leading from the ancient mysteries to the present, and onward to future tasks. ('Thomas is particularly close to me. Am deeply touched by this'.) On May 28, 1953 König noted that he had been working intensively with Rudolf Steiner's great Ephesus verse of April 22, 1924 since the early morning hours.[3] He then continued to write about Alix Roth who had supported him during his nighttime heart troubles and physical crises during those difficult years:

> Once again am deeply moved [by the Ephesus verse].
> As Alix sits at my bed, notice immediately in her facial expression that the two of us are connected from earlier times. Then suddenly I know the origin of the connection with my friends at the Clinic in Arlesheim and Dr Wegman, although our earthly paths separated. I went to Palestine, the others did not. Arabia followed, then the post-medieval world of the seventh century which was connected with the Bohemian brotherhood, and only now all these threads have come together again. The others went through the Orders (Dominican), I did not.

Nine years later, on June 17, 1962 König notes again:

> We have supper with Thomas [Weihs] and Ännchen
> [Anke] at St John's Cottage in the evening. Afterwards
> they show me their photo-album of their journey to
> Greece and am completely taken by the landscapes.
> Then go with Alix to the Hall and suddenly notice that
> the whole of Murtle is like Greece and a sense of a past
> time rises up in my soul.

A day later, on June 18, 1962, Karl König recorded a night
experience and described the spiritual background of Camphill
Hall. The hall, which was to be designed by König together with
Gabor Tallo and opened in and September, would become the
central community space for lectures and conferences, the organ
of the social Logos-activity, the 'Hall of Memory and
Conscience':

> Yesterday Alix unexpectedly asked me who had given me
> the plan for the hall. That was very surprising, as I had
> never asked the question myself. But yesterday when I
> felt that Murtle was like Greece, this sense fused with
> Alix's question and in the night it was revealed that
> Iphigenia had given the plan of the Hall to me. That is
> how the esoteric name of the Hall was found.[4] [Its
> second name is the Hall of Iphigenia.]

★

As early as 1939 Karl König had introduced ritual celebrations at
Kirkton House. These were the services given to the teachers of
the Waldorf School by Rudolf Steiner which were later also
handed over to Karl König by Ita Wegman. König emphasized
their central significance for the spiritual form of Camphill — in
reality he was actually pointing to the possibility of experiencing
the Christ and the Christ's activity.[5] After König's spiritual

Saturday January 24

Am Morgen mit den Ärzten den Film
über Temple-Fay's Methoden der Behand-
lung gelähmter Kinder gesehen. Es ist ent-
täuschend, obwohl sich Interessantes daran
demonstrieren lässt; vor allem der zwei-
takt aller Bewegung:

  Streckung — Ausatmung
  Beugung — Einatmung

  Darauf folgt eine lange & wichtige
Besprechung über Bewegung & die anzu-
wendenden Methoden bei gelähmten Kindern.

  In der Vorbereitung auf den Bibelabend
erscheint mir plötzlich die Nikodemus-Be-
gegnung wie ein erstes Aufleuchten dessen,
was „Reich Gottes" genannt wird. Diese
unendlich leise erstrahlende Atmosphäre,
in welcher der Auferstandene wandelt.
Das Heilige Land Shamballa wird für
Nikodemus beschrieben & dann als erster
von dem Nikodemus verbundenen
Freund Saulus betreten.

Diary entry of January 24, 1953. See page 81 for full translation.

experiences on the Isle of Man, where in a night experience Count Zinzendorf charged him to establish a Saturday evening meal when the Bible is read together, the weekly Bible Evenings also became part of essential community routines and work.[6] Every week König prepared intensively for the Bible Evening with the intention to attempt together to 'understand the [Gospel] text with the help of Rudolf Steiner's spiritual science.'[7] As the diaries show, during the Saturday gathering with friends König flourished in the same spiritually creative way that characterized his lecture preparation. This may be illustrated by his diary entries concerning the afternoon and evening of Easter Saturday, March 31, 1945, the last year of the war.

> Dictated a lot of correspondence, and then prepared for the Bible Evening. A great deal is revealed about the resurrection body. Recognize its nature and substance, and read *From Jesus to Christ* at length. Understand the transformation from body into head as an essential event in the phantom; and then at the Bible Evening, which is very beautiful, am able to speak of the Lamb as the white-haired one, the pure head that has emerged from the body. Attempt to try to write some of it down at night ...

In another entry on January 24, 1953, almost eight years later, he wrote:

> During preparation for the Bible Evening the Nicodemus encounter suddenly appears as a first dawning of what is called the 'Kingdom of God'. The infinitely soft, shining etheric sphere in which the Risen One walks. The Holy Land Shambala is described for Nicodemus and then is first entered by his friend, Saul.

In contrast, other diary entries show that König came to new insights during the conversations of the Bible Evening. Thus a spiritual community event took place within a spirit-filled,

Christ-centred dialogue ('Where two or three are gathered in my name, I am there amongst them.')

> Beautiful Bible Evening about the entry into Jerusalem. Many people make contributions, and in the process the deep relationship between the entry into Jerusalem and the moon forces becomes apparent to me. As there is an occult eclipse of the sun on Good Friday, so an occult eclipse of the moon took place there [on Palm Sunday]. The head is built as a Grail Temple. Will write some more afterwards. (March 24, 1945).

> At the Bible reading Alix and I speak at length about the conclusion of Chapter 21 of the Gospel of John. In the process the Risen One's threefold question to Peter can be seen as the threefold overcoming of the denials. Peter becomes the shepherd, that is, the guardian of the sacramental altar. John becomes the guardian of the cosmic communion. (May 14, 1955).

König regarded the Bible Evening to some extent as a communal contemplation of the actual events of the 'turning point in time.' ('Again [we] speak at length about Ascension. It is beautiful. And the feeling of Emmaus awakes strongly in my heart.' May 21, 1955.) Therefore he regarded it also as a context within which the specific ability to recall the Christ events could be developed, schooled and strengthened in each individual.

> Bible Evening in the chapel this evening. The friends do not say much. I try to describe the scene that takes place on the Mount of Olives where Christ speaks with the apostles about the future of the earth (the Little Apocalypse). The silence that descended that evening; at the foot, the Garden of Gethsemane and the apostles listening to the voice of the Logos. It is deeply moving to think that the Christ ascended into heaven from that

same place. If only all of this would live in us in an awake manner! How different we would all be. (Dec 3, 1955).

In similar vein, Karl König once wrote the following about the Camphill community.

> It is one of the principal tasks of the Community to make the reality of the Christ's life on earth so alive in each of its members, and those living and working within it, that each day of work and celebration is as though accompanied by Him. This should develop to the point where the landscapes of Palestine — Galilee and Judea — become a homeland for each one of us. Not that we engender a longing for it, but rather that this landscape is so engraved, so 'painted' within us that it becomes like the land of our youth. It ought to develop to the point where the days that Christ lived on earth, His words and actions, become like the garment of our souls and where our ways are guided by His ways.[8]

Rudolf Steiner's lectures on the *Fifth Gospel* were entirely orientated towards the 'turning point in time' and the 'facts of the life of Jesus Christ', and he had hoped that there would be a soul-spiritual understanding in his listeners, also with respect to the possibility of the individual ability to recall. ('It can be a help to these souls to remember the Mystery of Golgotha, to remember specific things that can then be researched in detail.'[9]) At the same time, however, Steiner's descriptions were a very specific kind of preparatory work for future tasks and development associated with the experience of the Christ in the etheric and the translation of these events into the social sphere.[10] In this sense, the Bible Evenings and the Sunday ritual celebrations were alive and active within both time streams and were a preparatory deed for future activity.[11]

> Am at Camphill for the Bible Evening. Speak about how
> the entry into Jerusalem is one of the most important
> images to be contemplated during our times; it describes
> the coming of the Christ in the etheric sphere, projects it
> forward in time, and is a kind of Christmas light.
> (April 10, 1954).
>
> The Bible Evening is not a ritual act; it is just the
> opposite. The Bible Evening is the loving preparation of
> the human soul for the experience of the cosmic
> communion.[12]

Karl König made it a priority to gradually clarify within the
Camphill community the deeper spiritual meaning of the Bible
Evening so that justice could be done to its reality and significance for the future.[13] His diary entries, however, repeatedly
show his deep satisfaction with the developments that had taken
place after only a few years. After a Bible Evening at Newton
Dee on April 3, 1954 he wrote:

> There are thirty friends at the Bible Evening. Experience
> just how many of them have changed and become more
> themselves. Have the clear impression that this has come
> about simply through the transformational power of the
> Bible Evenings, and this is a joyful experience. People
> become clearer, healthier and stronger in themselves.
> But that is 'the Good.'[14]

Time and again Karl König experienced very directly the
community-building aspect of the Bible Evening, and the possibility for certain realities to be revealed within this special context. Referring to this, he once said there should be a 'common
language' in the Camphill movement.[15] One and a half years following the previously-quoted diary entry, on October 4, 1955,
he wrote the following while at Thornbury in southern
England.

Thomas [Weihs] and Ännchen [Anke] arrive in the evening ... They are refreshing and bring life with them, and this is good for me. They say a lot about Camphill and Michaelmas. In the evening Thomas tells me that at the previous Bible Evening he knew exactly what I had been thinking, and then he describes exactly, almost with the same words, what I had expressed here about the twelfth chapter [of the Apocalypse]. It is deeply moving to know this.

★

Karl König's diary entries regarding the spiritual community-building process in Camphill also show how he continued to wrestle intensively with what was *not* being achieved and what was still necessary socially for a true brotherhood to be formed amongst themselves. 'Say that it would be good if we would try to live in such a way that the friend's faults are for each person the expression of their own faults' (June 29, 1943). König endeavoured to achieve this — at times, an extraordinarily tiring process for him — at conferences. 'The whole process extends well beyond the afternoon, but it is not inspired; it is as if dust and tiredness were covering everything.' (June 29, 1956) In almost daily conversations with many colleagues he gave advice, positive support and his understanding of each unique situation. 'In the afternoon I speak with a number of colleagues and manage to straighten out a few things. I am again presented with the infinite variety of human beings and how much tact and understanding is needed if one wants to meet their needs.' (March 27, 1954).[16] Despite the high cost to his strength, König welcomed many of the community meetings and individual encounters — in this way the community spirit came to the fore and the positive developments of individuals could be recognized. A diary entry on January 3, 1953, a Sunday, illustrates this.

Unusually satisfying conversations with some colleagues in the afternoon and the effects of the blessing of Camphill were evident in some individual human destinies. The saying, 'Here is a human school,' strengthened in me more and more, and I was filled with a strong feeling of joyful gratitude.

At the same time the diary entries also show clearly how their author constantly suffered from the fact that the community — both individual colleagues and the combined whole — could not sustain the necessary level of soul-spiritual development. 'At the conference am again deeply affected by the lethargy and lack of will' (Feb 2, 1944). 'Deeply saddening to see this paralysis and lack of willingness to sacrifice' (Feb 3, 1944).

While Karl König persistently cultivated consciousness of the Christian esoteric task of Camphill in the light of the Foundation Stone Meditation, under the sign of the 'Divine Light' and the coming of the 'Christ Sun' in the etheric, he also saw the dangers of possible failure — a repetition of the apostles' sleep at Gethsemane, the lack of spirit awareness and the lack of capacity to sacrifice. König carried this insight with positivity and all his available strength:

> ... Spent a long time with the friends and again discussed tasks and problems. Must tell them that they are still too much asleep and therefore unable to see Camphill's needs in the right way. Nevertheless, a good conversation. Much insight gained and many good efforts to improve things. (Jan 2, 1957)

In times of great community crisis or his own depressions Karl König wrote about Camphill's imminent failure and considered the co-workers too weak to be able solve the impending tasks. 'In fact, all the work here at Camphill is condemned to collapse. It is too powerful for the people of today and will not hold together.' (Aug 21, 1943). At the same time he experienced the concerns, difficulties and needs of individuals as part of the all-embracing task and special radiating warmth of Camphill. In his eyes, this was a community of helpers, themselves also in need of help and support.

> Our co-workers are an ailing group of people! But how would they find themselves if not here at Camphill? And what would our children do without the many who are almost the same as they are? It is a cross that we must continue to bear. (Jan 4, 1963).

While König wrestled constantly with the egotistic desires of various colleagues, at the same time he acknowledged the extent of the social demands Camphill placed on people and recognized the individual difficulties underlying complaints, weaknesses and mistakes. For a long time König willingly carried responsibility for the success of the whole, created social forms which could become increasingly independent of him and the karmically-related founding group.[17] He tried to meet, where possible, the expectations of the individual co-workers in their specific circumstances, while at the same time protecting the spirit of Camphill. 'How can one satisfy *all* private wishes and still keep Camphill going?' (June 24, 1957). During this long process Camphill and its community went though countless trials. Human relationships and bonds disintegrated ('It is so destructive when such separation shocks arise and undermine the progress of our work' June 18, 1956) and many challenges could not be overcome satisfactorily despite all König's efforts. At one time König noted questioningly about a colleague:

> The restlessness of modern life, bad behaviour and the inability to keep inner and outer order is a central theme in this life. Why doesn't anthroposophy take effect and take hold more deeply?

★

Although Camphill's public presence grew, and many people flocked to the community, Karl König remained persistently vigilant and critical. In his colleagues he often missed the open-mindedness and world interest that was so characteristic of him. König's cosmopolitan orientation brought him into contact with many people in cultural, scientific and public life, thus introducing Camphill to the wider world. 'Everything ... is very stiff, inflexible and unfree. No sign of a man-of-the-world. ... All the Camphillers are extremely arrogant.' (Jan 24, 1956). Despite significant progress within the community, Karl König continued to be concerned about the future of the therapeutic and social work. Following a guest tour through the entire estate, he noted in his diaries on August 14 and 15, 1954:

> Go to Heathcot in the morning to welcome a group of Norwegian physiotherapists who have come to visit the school; Dr Munck and the painter are here to visit. Am together with them during the day and it is interesting for me to go through all the houses as a kind of visitor. Heathcot, Camphill and Murtle are still extremely impressive but Newton Dee and Cairnlee seem very depressing, and I have a very bad feeling although the visitors are very positive.
>
> Am tired and dejected when I return to Camphill, but do not know what was so bad that I should become negatively inclined.
>
> Am too tired to go to the Bible Evening and stay at my desk without anything particular to do.
> (Aug 14, 1954)

> When I wake up in the morning it becomes clear that yesterday I did not meet the something that is essential to Camphill, namely that the children participate in the adults' work and are enthusiastically and socially occupied. Yesterday I hardly saw a child who was truly working; they were well cared for, but the spiritual

family that should be together in work was not alive there. The effect was depressing and I am now crushed and also so physically tired that I can hardly move from my room.

Had conversations and negotiations in the afternoon but the bitter dejection will not abate. In the evening go directly to bed. (Aug 15, 1954)

Despite countless traces of depression and dejection in König's diary entries, these were seldom underscored with true bitterness or pervaded by accusations. More often the tone sounding was one of the concerned question, the wish to get to the bottom of a problem and the conscious examination of paths already taken.[18] Thus during a visit to Glencraig in Northern Ireland on February 3, 1965, a year before his death, he wrote:

Meet all the villagers for tea in the afternoon and become aware of many problems. Some have become so terribly old and fragile. Why? Why has the institutional atmosphere not been transformed here? Is it wrong to have the school and village together? Am truly distraught by these thoughts and observations, but for the time being will not say anything about it. We are still so much at the beginning of it all.

Seven weeks later, at Brachenreuthe in southern Germany he wrote:

Today is a day of consultations. In the morning and afternoon the parents visit with or without their adult children, seeking advice and admission to Lehenhof. Experience in conversation how inadequate our work is and how deficient and unskilled the co-workers often are. It is painfully clear now that here in Germany something entirely different is expected from a village

Floris Books

Name (BLOCK CAPS): _____

Address: _____

_____

Postcode: _____ Country: _____

Email: _____
if you want to receive information this way

☐ Please send me the Floris Books complete catalogue once

Please make sure I'm on the Floris Books mailing list to receive information on (please tick):

*We will **never** pass your details to anyone else*

Religion and Spirituality

☐ AA Christian Spirituality
☐ AB Bible
☐ AC World Spirituality
☐ AD Celtic Spirituality
☐ AE Science & Spirituality
☐ H Philosophy
☐ D Art & Architecture

☐ C Mind Body Spirit
  ☐ CA Holistic Health
☐ B Self-help
☐ G Organics, Biodynamics & Sustainable Living
☐ I Steiner-Waldorf Education
☐ IA Steiner Teacher Resources
☐ IB Special Needs Education

☐ J Child Health & Development
☐ L Activities and Crafts with children *(all ages)*
☐ K Picture Books *(age 3-7)*
  ☐ KA Elsa Beskow Books
☐ M Story Books *(age 6-10)*
☐ NB Kelpies novels *(age 8-12)*

Floris Books
15 Harrison Gardens
Edinburgh EH11 1SH
UK

Floris Books

estate than those in the more westerly regions. In the future it must be possible to integrate psychiatric cases. But how would that be managed? (March 26, 1965).

Only two weeks later, he again wrote, 'If only Camphill had more strength to support all these destinies! But we are also too weak.' (April 10, 1965).

★

König's diaries were also often permeated with joy and delight in what had been achieved despite all the difficulties: delight in his colleagues, who, in their way, delivered outstanding work and who continually gave everything possible to do justice to Camphill's spiritual task. 'At lunchtime Thomas [Weihs] is with me for a long time and tells me in detail about Norway. He was able to accomplish everything in an amazingly wise and mature way and I am very happy about that. Different to how I would have done it, yet still completely within the Camphill way.' (March 17, 1955). König experienced that the many weaknesses notwithstanding, the spiritual community still survived and carried the spirit of the Camphill movement. Camphill had indeed become a shining entity, soul-receptive and soul-supporting. 'Sense that Camphill has become a spiritual space in which many searching souls can find their home. That is a great gift.' (Sep 25, 1955).

Following a tour of Botton on March 27, 1963 König noted:

Go through the workshops and see the puppet production, the weaving and glass workshop and many other things. Am amazed over and over. Everything that has been achieved and developed here, and continues to develop, is like a miracle.

At Camphill, three days later, he wrote:

Today is the thirty-eighth anniversary of Rudolf Steiner's death. The rain is streaming down outside and it is also bitterly cold. Drive to the Hall where the service is being held by Alix [Roth], Ännchen [Anke Weihs] and Gisela [Schlegel]. Am overwhelmed with amazement at how everything has turned out: The hall, the three women at the altar, the many people united in the service. This is extraordinary.

5

Knowing and Supporting the Children

Morning at Heathcot. See the children and massage Leila. I know that I must find out more about her illness so that we can continue to help her. A task for the coming year is to heal this child who lives as a saint.

(Jan 2, 1945)

Karl König undertook a large number of tasks during his life. Stimulated and guided by Rudolf Steiner's life work, König not only followed new research paths in medicine, education and curative education, biology, astrology, agriculture, social and religious life, but also in art and literature, music and architecture. At the centre of all this, however — and at the core of Camphill, the spiritual community that had come into being through König — was the concern for the child with special needs. This included diagnosis based on research and deeper insight, and unconditional therapeutic support of the charges entrusted to him. On November 22, 1962 he wrote in his diary:

> In conversation it becomes clear to me that the friends
> are searching for something else instead of being satisfied
> with what they have. And it seems to me that for our
> work in this country it is essential now to become calm

and not to run after phantoms, to deepen the work with the children, and to reflect again on the fundamental impulses of curative education. This is the insight that comes to me.

Karl König had come to Arlesheim through paediatric medicine, and from there, with Ita Wegman's encouragement, he found his way to Sonnenhof. 'Since then these people have been my *raison d'être.*'[1] This path led Karl König to Tilla Maasberg, Silesia and Bohemia, and later to the landscapes of Irish-Scottish Christianity and the Templars before he returned to Central Europe and Lake Constance, an area he considered to be spiritually linked to Ephesus.[2] König had united himself with a therapeutic Christian stream which formed its central task around the child with special needs — often enough with their decisive help — under the star of Kaspar Hauser and in intensive encounter with the destructive powers of the twentieth century.[3]

The early years of Camphill were difficult, demanding all of Karl König's available strength, courage and determination. Particularly during 1943, the year of Ita Wegman's death, König encountered the greatest challenges — during the time of the culmination of war, the months after the Stalingrad battle and the year Hans and Sophie Scholl (of the White Rose resistance movement) were executed and when hundreds of thousands of soldiers fell. Co-workers left the young community and the first child died under König's care, despite all his efforts. On April 14, 1943 he wrote in his diary:

> Woken at 6.30 AM, Sandy Thomson is very ill. Go to Cottage. Peter comes towards me and says: 'He is dead'. Find Sandy lifeless. Still try to revive him. It is no use. Go back and tell Tilla. Lay out his body. Dr Shand comes in the morning. Then the police and an 'inquest' is held for hours ...

It is a dreadful day. In the evening we read for Sandy — the third lecture from the cycle, *Christ and the Spiritual World*. Destiny has struck.

The following day König began his diary entry with the words, 'As if paralysed this morning.' On April 18, only five days later König wrote, 'Telephone call, Alan is having a seizure. Drive to Eidda House. Am able to help save him. Back at 10.30. Then very late evening meal with everyone.'

During these months Karl König accompanied the children and the Camphill community day and night, constantly concerned about their wellbeing. 'Wake up at 3 AM in the night, full of anxiety. Think that Marianne is in danger. Ask Alix to look in at the Cottage. All is peaceful there ... Later Marianne says she felt stressed during the night.' July 26, 1943). On July 27, König noted: 'Up in the night at 3 AM again, filled with anxiety. Do not know what to do. But then poor Sandy Smith stands naked at the door. I know the children call.'

Also during this time illnesses struck Camphill, interfering with the work and increasing pressure and worry. On August 27, König entrusted the following observation to his diary: 'The children are somewhat better and the day more peaceful. Am tired and very depressed. As if there was an epidemic of my guilt, and perhaps it really is so.'

Almost four weeks later, the following entry: 'At home in the morning and then saw children. The homeopathy is getting there progressively and helps a great deal. But sense my ignorance very deeply.' (Sep 23, 1943).

Finally, on October 26, he wrote, 'Feel thoroughly wretched and have the impression I have failed completely as a doctor.'

★

In times of great difficulty, Karl König and Camphill repeatedly received crucial help from both inner and outer sources. In

1943 the figure of Kaspar Hauser appears noticeably in Karl König's diaries. König had already made a comprehensive study of this figure during the Pilgramshain period, the same year that had begun with intensive work on Rudolf Steiner's Curative Education Course and was very consciously concluded with a study of Friedrich Schiller. 'Still much unease and fear about sleeping. Very drawn to Schiller and read about him.' (Dec 13, 1943). 'Worked on Schiller and read about him. Very moved.' (Dec 14, 1943). 'Read much about Schiller and *The Bell* is revealed as a heart form. Then experience Schiller's spirit behind the Youth Circle. Deeply moved by the harmony of the two horoscopes. Thus his heart beats in us when ours has developed enough.' (Dec 18, 1943). 'Feel how important his relevance is for us.' (Dec 25, 1943). 'Show the deeds of Michael and their expression in Schiller's plays. (Dec 28, 1943).[4]

König followed an inner path almost entirely of threshold experiences which he had clearly set for himself, and then had to overcome within his exposed, unconventional life and his trust in the spiritual world. This pressure and the wider tensions of the Second World accompanied Camphill's steps and the development of therapy and support processes for the children.

> In the night from June 23 to 24, the following happened at Heathcot:
> Christine, who is completely paralysed, had also been sleeping in Janet's room. In the evening she was very agitated and so Janet took her into her room. In the middle of the night Christine wakes up and screams. Janet gets up and tries to calm the child. Janet becomes more and more anxious and thinks she must take the child into bed with her — something that she never does. As Christine lies next to her, there is a terrible crash and rumbling (like a bomb, Janet said afterwards)

and the oak shelf of crystals and heavy stones falls down, directly onto Christine's bed. If she had been lying there she would have been killed. The spiritual powers watch over their charges. (June 24, 1945).

Karl König's occasionally depressed and self-doubting, or even despairing diary entries during the 1940s ('deep sense of my ignorance') should not obscure the fact that by this time he was already a highly-skilled doctor with immense clinical experience and exceedingly unusual capacities for diagnosis and therapy, who was sought after by tens of thousands of patients in Silesia. König's notes from the Pilgramshain years show the intensive way in which he already had profound insights into illnesses and handicaps. He deepened and integrated these opinions and insights into the diagnostic-therapeutic work over the following years. More and more children were introduced to König in the post-war years in Scotland and also during his many travels. On March 18, 1954 he wrote:

During the day I see many children and this time not one of them comes with the correct diagnosis. Am deeply touched by some of the children and their needs, and know why this work is so necessary.

With regard to the anthroposophical curative education König's goal — corresponding, and indeed identical to Rudolf Steiner's — included the attainment of clear knowledge of the incarnation and destiny of a child as an essential precondition for every aspect of further medical and educational support provided.[5] Karl König's demands on himself in this regard were boundless, and his diaries were again the place of continual self-reflection and self-criticism where he became aware of what had been successful, what was missing and what still had to be attained in the future. On January 12, 1953 he wrote:

Clinic for the first time again after the so-called holiday, but although I saw extraordinary children, their characters did not remain with me and did not take on a form within me.

A day later, on January 13, 1953, he already wrote more optimistically:

When I came to Murtle after the clinic, it was better and the children revealed themselves more strongly than the previous day. I had a clear supersensible impression of Cynthia.

Again one and a half years later, on June 2, 1954, König addresses the same issue with regard to his consultations in London in a restrained but self-critical manner:

See children and parents again in the morning and afternoon, and it is the same as yesterday. I can see a little more deeply, and am able to come a little closer to the essence of the incarnation. Sense a few things about the cooperation between parent and child destinies, but it does not become concrete.

In the immediately following days, he continued with the following words:

The parents and children are there again in the afternoon and it is remarkable and strange how one must often go step-by-step through trials in meeting these children's destinies and the parents' fate. It takes strength but it also gives strength, and when there is enough wakefulness something happens in these conversations and meetings that I can only describe as cathartic. This only becomes clear to me through writing about it; I did not know this before. (June 3, 1954).

During the day I see children again; try to be silent and objective, but these are particularly strange destinies that have come together here this morning. It will take longer to come to the right catharsis. (June 4, 1954).

In the course of his many travels, König experienced on a large scale the variations and typology of many illnesses and handicaps. 'As always, it is strange to become conscious of the stature of these children internationally and to experience how they show the same disturbances and problems all over the world' (Feb 10, 1954). König studied international specialist literature and continually endeavoured to stay abreast of the most recent research. This enormous efforts to gain knowledge led to countless publications and scientific papers, but more importantly benefitted the children in the form of social support and consistent therapeutic improvements.

In the morning, once again a whole succession of children; I admit some of them. When I stand in front of these parents and children, I experience over and over again an affirmation of myself and the work; as if this truly is the work I have assigned to myself. The children feel understood and the parents are comforted and received into the realm of humanness. (July 6, 1954).

This day is completely devoted to clinical examinations of a number of children. Mainly see new children, still unknown to me, and record very clearly some of the deeper disturbances. Many glimpses into the essential nature of the children emerge in the process and therefore recommendations can be made. (Oct 9, 1956).

See children the whole day, almost without a break. They are very interesting children, somehow different to ours at Camphill and some are real hard nuts to crack. But very encouraging to find the right starting point for each child, and thereby the necessary therapy. (Glencraig, July 5, 1957).

At the Clinic I see new children and again receive strong impressions of their condition and appearance. Am able to understand a great deal and can explain this to the doctors. It is a real demonstration lesson, and I gain many insights. (March 16, 1953).

Am once again at Heathcot for the Clinic in the morning and see two children. Their condition is immediately clearly visible to me and am able to describe these in an understandable way; somehow heartening to have such a clear understanding of the children and am happy about that. (Sep 1, 1953).

Speak for a long time with Ilse [Rascher] about a deaf and blind child and try to show her that in his case (tubercular meningitis) the tactile area of the eye has been lost. That is why he is blind and cannot distinguish between objects anymore — not because the ability to sense light is missing. Thus there are new prospects for treatment. (Dec 4, 1955).

Karl König was extremely pleased — indeed, almost happy — when the necessary steps in coming to diagnostic and therapeutic insights were successfully completed together with his colleagues and when those involved were united in their approach; that is, when they were a community acting out of insight, in the sense of Michaelic Christianity:

Am at Newton Dee in the morning, and together with Marianne Sander we go through the boys that she has for speech therapy. She presents each child to me, shows me what she does and then we discuss the basis of the disturbance and possible adjustments to treatment. Encountering speech in such an immediate way makes a strong impression on me and it is once again completely clear that the archetypes of speech disturbances may be found in the different forms of paralysis. (Dec 12, 1956).

Hold a 'clinic' with the friends the whole morning and early afternoon. We see every single child that has been admitted to Helgeseter and discuss in detail the necessary educational and medical interventions. Again it is a great joy to be able to recognize each child's unique incarnation form and to be able to develop the necessary treatment with the help of this knowledge. We are all united in our enthusiasm about what we are able to discover here. (Aug 30, 1954).

On the other hand, König's entries could be more critical and incisive regarding the aims of the work, as in this excerpt written after a school celebration at Glencraig in northern Ireland.

All children show what they have learned and it is very enlightening to see how amateurish much of the work actually still is. After lunch I sit together with the friends and discuss this at length with them. The children have not yet been 'recognized' in their essence thoroughly and therefore they have not yet been 'redeemed.' Thus our specific task in curative education reveals itself to me: To redeem the true essence of the human being through cognition. (March 24, 1956).

It should not be underestimated that in this respect and in relation to his aims Karl König was frequently disappointed and had to experience that his medical, therapy and education colleagues — including highly talented personalities — could only partially keep up with him. He had to learn over and again that in spite of his own rigorous process, he only succeeded to some extent in explaining his methods of observing the sense-perceptible and supersensory to his medical colleagues.

There is a clinic here at Camphill this morning. See a series of particularly interesting children, can say much about them because I may see through into their conditions. Now the situation is such that I have great certainty in diagnosing and that the smallest signs give me the strongest insights. But it is not possible to teach all of this. (Nov 27, 1956).

In this regard, König also wrote on March 10, 1954:

We have a clinic at Thornbury House in the morning and afternoon, and I give a kind of demonstration showing the type of children who must be seen and understood. But lethargic thinking still prevents the friends from helping themselves. The very sight of a child seems to paralyse them.

Although during the following years Karl König's methods of instruction became more effective, he continued to the very end of his life to be self-critical and self-questioning about processes of development that were often inadequate and unsuccessful. While in such circumstances he experienced a failure in the common task, he shouldered sole responsibility:

There is a clinic at Murtle in the morning. There is new heartbreak: the epileptic children who are growing up, Oliver Murdoch and Leslie Talbot, are overwhelmed by puberty and engulfed by their bodies. Why are we unable to solve this problem? Many of the children deteriorate because of our incompetence. (March 31, 1954)

At the same time König often raised the question of making basic changes based on renewed consideration of the unique destiny of each individual, so that — even with the maximum 'will to heal' — they would be continually recognized and respected anew.

Tuesday March 10

Vormittags halte ich Clinic im Park & bin sehr beeindruckt von den Fortschritten, die die Kinder während der letzten Monate gemacht haben. Das ist eine große Freude & es erscheinen die „Cerebral Palsy"- Kinder in einem neuen Licht. Spasticity, Rigidity, Athetose sind nicht nur ein Zustand der Muskulatur, sondern ein Seelen"- Zustand, der tief in die Temperament-Sphäre eingreift; erst wenn das erkannt wird, bekommt das ganze Problem sein wahres Gesicht.

Mittags überkommt mich dann eine außerordentliche Schwäche; ich sehe noch Kinder, die von auswärts angemeldet sind, muß aber dann mich hinlegen.

Lese manches, aber die Schwäche ist übergroß & lähmt mich. Ich gehe mit Angst in den Schlaf.

Diary entry of March 10, 1953. See page 81 for translation.

In the morning at Murtle for a clinic. Saw new and old
children and experienced and felt many strange things in
the process. Can we really help in a decisive way? Or
does the personality structure not remain completely
beyond influence, and must it not do this? We must
actually learn to understand the endless variety of
individualities so that they may be enabled to find their
place in life.' (Oct 26, 1956).

On the other hand Karl König could be joyfully surprised and
touched by the unexpected, positive therapeutic changes that he
perceived. On May 23, 1956 he wrote:

In the morning, have a very positive feeling about the
work here and then hold a clinic. But beforehand still
went through the individual classes and am very moved
by the progress that I find in some of the children. This
is far more than I would ever have dared to hope for two
years ago.

★

In the midst of all the failures and successes, however, right to
the end Karl König experienced the misery and need, compas-
sion and deep despair in the destiny of the person before him,
and for this he made himself unconditionally available in the
spirit of early Christianity and its culture of conscious selfless-
ness which belongs in the future. In 1914, at the beginning of
the First World War, Steiner described how humanity will only
be fully present when it is possible for single individuals to experience *within themselves* the real pain of their fellow human
beings. He subsequently said:

Here I would like to point to a far distant ideal. The
great Ideal of humanity will only come into being in full

measure when it becomes impossible for the pain of one *not* to be felt by the others also. ...

It is a great, though far off ideal, that not only the sick or injured one feels the pain, but that others feel it just as acutely. This is really the Christ Ideal.[6]

Karl König accomplished his therapeutic life path and the founding of the Camphill community in the light of this ideal and through the active endeavour to bring it about in an initial form in the present.

König's heart-mind-medicine came to life and lived out of the substance of the Fifth Gospel and the Christ-ideal identified by Rudolf Steiner, even in those instances where, despite all efforts, he still experienced it as inadequate:

> During the day I see children and parents. Again and again I am overwhelmed by the suffering in these destinies that are unresolved and often insoluble. Over and over, our lack of knowledge, our confused social order and people's blindness about these problems destroys the active help. Seeds must be planted individually, in small circles, and it is to be hoped that they can carry more and more fruit. (Feb 17, 1953).

> See one of the bigger boys who has been spoilt by so-called anthroposophical curative education. Then a very seriously ill, blind and disturbed child and various other people. It is a procession of suffering, sacrifice and sincerity that triggers nothing but compassion and the will to help. (April 13, 1965).

> A full day of people today. Consultations in the morning and afternoon. See much misery, stubbornness and real suffering. Notice — as so often — how incapable we are as human beings of accomplishing what is required of

us. Objectivity with respect to the self is missing.
(May 7, 1965).

I am growing fearful of the sheer numbers of destinies
which are presented to me every day, demanding answers
... How will my heart, which has become greatly over-
tired, be able to survive it all? (Nov 24, 1965).

Translation of Diary Facsimiles

Wednesday, May 25, 1955 (p. 16)

The night was not too bad, and despite of the fact that I did not sleep through, I feel quite refreshed. After the morning meditation, again negative thoughts and feelings well up that make me feel cynical and without hope. Then I read an article — not a very remarkable one — of Prof J. Wach, 'Modern Man's Self Conception.' When he discusses the inherent encounter between God and man, shackles fall off my heart and something begins to stir, which I can formulate towards the evening. It begins with the words, 'You may know everything,' and tries to show that not only spiritual science is required, but a direct experience of God. I am full of remorse about my errors.

Wednesday, February 4, 1953 (p. 26)

When I wake up in the morning and open the curtain I experience something very significant: that the eye is not for seeing things and objects but to prepare the space in which the things and objects 'can let themselves become visible.' Then I experience how the light penetrated me through the eye. Through this I could take part in a space of light which was spreading out around me. Through this space created by the eye — like a candle which is lit in the darkness — the objects in this space appeared and compelled me to perceive them.

Then I looked at the Raphael cartoons, especially the one 'Feed my Sheep' which is so wonderfully alive.

In the afternoon [I see] children. Although they are very interesting, I have little inner participation and insight.

Wednesday, May 18, 1955 (p. 31)

Today is Gustav Mahler's death day and I am somehow directed by this during the morning. He died forty-four years ago, quite young still but perfect. I read in Alma's book about this death and pick up the beautiful photograph which I have of him.

In the evening I listen to the Second Symphony together with Alix. It is beautiful and moving to experience this masterpiece again. I then remember the dream which I had after having visited his grave. It was revealed to me that this symphony represents nothing else, but the Raising of Lazarus.

Indeed, this it is, and perchance Mahler was present then and experienced it again.

Otherwise there is not much of importance. I see Morwenna who tells me at length about Cairnlee. Then I read a very important article by Prof Haubold about Down's syndrome which has just appeared.

Saturday, February 21, 1953 (p. 34)

In the morning I try to prepare myself for the coming lectures, especially about: A new approach to sense perception. It is difficult to gain the right inspiration and so cobble something together what I anyway know and made a kind of lecture of it and feel very ashamed.

There are many people present and I begin to speak and the 'spirit wind' begins to blow; but in the middle of the lecture it grows silent around me and only with effort do I formulate the words and feel an unfathomable emptiness. I look on myself as from outside and see myself struggle like a fish on dry land. But I am able to finish speaking.

The second lecture about 'smelling and tasting' is much better. It is filled and I am astonished how alive and spirit-filled I am allowed to speak. The experience of grace and thankfulness is great, in the evening Michael Wilson speaks. Afterwards I am so tired that I am unable to partake in the Bible Evening.

Wednesday, December 9, 1953 (p. 41)

I am again able to write and continue where I had to stop last week. I attempt to describe the three spaces, the visible space, the audible space and the tactile space and to explain vertigo as the result of an alteration of the relationship of these three spaces. This throws light on the structure of the skull, and relates the three spaces to the skull cavity, vestibular apparatus, and eye muscles. Thereby is revealed the threefold structure of the sense of balance. In the skull it is 'head' like, in the semicircular canals it is 'rhythmical system', and in the muscles of the eyes it is metabolic/limb system.

I then work out, without writing it down, how the legs, in particular the thighs metamorphose into the eyes and the middle ear into the arms.

This task is growing over my head and I have to be careful not to be overwhelmed.

Sunday, September 20, 1953 (p. 45)

In the morning I start to write and make a little progress. Then I read in Eugen Kolisko's essay on druids and bards. I sense why he had to die at Paddington Station. Trains leave from there to the west, to Wales, Tintagel, Glastonbury and Penmaenmawr. Now I can write and tell what I feel is important in this mysterious life.

Now it becomes obvious also why he chose to incarnate in Vienna. He needed to immerse himself into a musical atmosphere in order that his musical soul of a bard did not feel too lonely in this modern time.

When I lay down my pen in the evening I am satisfied. I am again aware who deeply I am connected with his destiny. This is much consolation in the present distress and emptiness of soul.

At 7.30 little Andrew Paton died at the hospital, the last child of the measles epidemic brought to [hospital in] Aberdeen a few days ago.

Saturday, January 24, 1953 (p. 54)

In the morning I watched with the doctors the film about Temple-Faye's methods of treatment of paralytic children. It was disappointing, although one can demonstrate interesting aspects by it, in particular the twofold rhythm of all movement.

> extension — exhale
> bending — inhale

Then follows a long and important discussion and movement and the methods to be used in treating paralytic children

While preparing for the Bible Evening the meeting of Christ with Nicodemus suddenly appears to me to be the first glow of what is called 'the kingdom of heaven.' This infinitely subtle etheric sphere in which the Risen One dwells.

The holy land Shamballa is described by Nicodemus, and his friend, Saul, is the first who enters it.

Tuesday, March 10, 1953 (p. 76)

During the morning we have clinic in [Thornbury] Park and I am impressed with the progress the children have made during the last few months. This is a great joy; the spastic children appear in a new light. Spasticity, rigidity and athetosis are not only a condition of the muscles, but also of the soul, and have a deep influence on the realm of the temperament. Only when this is recognized do we begin to understand these conditions.

At noon I suddenly feel very weak. I still can see some of the children who have come in from further away, but then I have to withdraw and lay down.

I read a bit, but the weakness robs all my strength and paralyses me. I fall asleep with anxiety.

Notes

HMW is Hans Müller-Wiedemann, *Karl König, a Central European Biography of the Twentieth Century.*

Introduction

1 Erhard Fucke, *Siebzehn Begegnungen.* p. 86.

2 Peter Roth, Foreword to Karl König's *Plays,* p. 5.

3 HMW, p. 438.

4 HMW, p. 91

5 Hans Müller-Wiedemann commented on König's diary entries in the following general way: 'All the indications are that König kept a diary throughout his conscious life. He was not only a person of considerable power and substance but also a writer by nature. Both his letters and above all his unpublished writings testify to this: notes on Steiner's lectures, reflections about himself and meetings with others, as well as notes on his own studies and some profound reflections on the Bible, which König probably read every day. The diaries also contain preparations for the lectures that he gave (for the most part worked out in detail), together with notes about inner experiences which found expression in poems, poetic prose and above all in his plays. Throughout his life König made diary-like notes in greater or lesser detail by way of preparation for his lectures, almost always accompanied by drawings or diagrams of one kind or another.

What has remained of König's diaries contains evidence of a life's path which was reflected to a surprisingly large extent in his solitary struggle between the destiny-bearing spiritual powers and his own soul. Especially in the early days of Camphill, hardly a day went by without a substantial note or diary entry, and we may gather from the notes in particular what he felt himself called upon to contribute in order that the Community might flourish. König made these entries in what were for the most part beautifully bound books which Tilla gave him, or in desk diaries with words from the works of Steiner by way of introduction. This he would write on the first page, and accompany it with a photograph of Rudolf Steiner. The early diaries include probing questions concerning his tasks in the Community and reflections, often of a painful kind, about his own failures, as well as his struggles with his bodily nature which accompanied him throughout his life. This shows his ethos of not using his diaries merely for the purpose of reporting but, using all the strength available to him, to give account of what he had recognized, and for finding strict criteria for his own activity through written reflection.' (HMW, pp. 323f).

6 It is envisaged that to encompass diary entries relevant to the stages of development of König's various books and essays, to his travels, to individual biographies of spiritual-historical personalities and to music. They will be accompanied with commentary.

7 In my opinion the most outstanding literary portrait of Karl König may be found in the phenomenologically developed chapter, 'Personal and more than personal' (HMW, pp. 309–30), including Anke Weihs' descriptions of König quoted therein.

8 Karl König, in words of the Foundation Stone of Camphill Hall (July 1, 1961). The complete formulation reads: 'Through Rudolf Steiner, mankind's leader in our century, the way to the Spirit was shown to us. Him we will follow:

> In willing the good
> In recognizing he truth,
> In loving the Christ.'

9 See my books, *Rudolf Steiner und das Fünfte Evangelium*. Dornach 2005, and *Die Kultur der Selbstlosigkeit*. Dornach 2006.

Chapter 1

1 Karl König, *Ewige Kindheit*, p. 2.

2 In a diary entry of October 4, 1965, less than six months before his death, Karl König wrote in retrospect about the train journey he had taken from Basel to Lausanne the same day: 'There is a man in the compartment who is as small as I am, and I have to think about what it means for people such as ourselves to be incarnated in such a form.'

3 'The existential feeling of being a refugee, homeless and, moreover, a Jew, never left him.' (HMW, p. 319).

4 Compare the report by the younger (by one year) Fritz Götte who experienced König's early appearances at the Goetheanum and in Germany. Four decades later he wrote his recollections: 'When König appeared among us — I first experienced him in Stuttgart nearly forty years ago — he proved himself from the outset to be an outstanding teacher. He seemed so certain and prescient that at the time we did not think of him as a contemporary of ours, and certainly not that this 24-year old had only been a member of our Society for just over a year.

Destiny decreed that König took this step into our circles on the day of Rudolf Steiner's death, March 30, 1925. At that time he was giving lectures at the Goetheanum on the development of the human embryo, lectures in which he claimed to recognize the great stages of world evolution from Saturn in the embryonic blastula-morula-gastrula stage. A pronounced Aristotelian line of thinking had emerged. The impression made on those at the Goetheanum was considerable. But — doubtless because boundaries had been overstepped — opposition soon stirred, and the young scholar found himself becoming entangled in all manner of problems. In hindsight I must admit that the young Karl König furnished an example of a remark which Rudolf Steiner made in 1923 to a circle of thirty people in Stuttgart: 'This is what I have explained as the system of inner opposition. Talents must be placed at the service of the cause rather than work against it! ... Talents are often highly uncomfortable.' Karl König was indeed highly creative, but on that account also 'uncomfortable.' (HMW, p. 71).

5 For a more complete spiritual background of this subject see my study *Die Kultur der Selbstlosigkeit.*

6 With regard to König's deep and primary *social* concern and his predominantly critical relationship to the Anthroposophical Society see HMW, pp. 45ff. The Society was incapable of bringing 'the revelations of the Christ impulse in our time into social life' (HMW, p. 196). At the end of lengthy descriptions, Müller-Wiedemann wrote, among other things:

Although König belonged to the beginning of the age of Michael, his visions had their focus far in the future of this age, in the sixth cultural epoch, which he endeavoured consciously to prepare for in various forms of community. The 'bourgeois state of sleep' of which Rudolf Steiner spoke in connection with the second half of the nineteenth century, and which continues today in different forms and dimensions, was from the outset an object of König's concern; and wherever a hint of this attitude ... appeared in his surroundings it brought about very strong reactions in him. Although those on the receiving end were doubtless not always aware of this, many of the choleric outburst from König's early days could be traced back to this deep sensitivity with regard to a far-reaching historical omission in the unfolding of central European consciousness in the second half of the nineteenth century, an omission which was caused by this attitude. Moreover, König had a deep sense of every individual's significance in the course of historical development, and judged human attitudes and failures in that light. Many who have grasped this have thereby gained a new consciousness of self, of being in a Christian sense not mere onlookers but participants in the world process. 'Only through being fully awake in spiritual-scientific experience can anything be achieved' (Rudolf Steiner) (HMW, p. 62)

König's diary entries of March 29, 1953 (the night before the 28th anniversary of Rudolf Steiner's death) where he wrote the content of his evening lecture, show his attitude — still in 1953 — in judging the social failures he had experienced in his contact with anthroposophy:

In the evening I try to speak about Rudolf Steiner in a way that I present him as a working man who wanted to bring anthroposophy into the social sphere. But the bourgeoisie always wanted to possess spiritual science and did not allow it to become what it should have become. Eurythmy was not brought into the factories, the Waldorf schools have become gentrified, over and again the Anthroposophical Society becomes a choir, and instead of ensuring that something healing enters humanity from the good impulses of the proletariat, egoism and vanity have grown. Thus the threefold social idea also had to collapse, and the same gentlemen who allowed it to collapse will continue to lead.'

Three weeks later, during a visit to Germany, König wrote: 'When will the anthroposophists be capable of bringing teaching and being into harmony? Why is it that what they think does not become reality?' (April 18, 1953)

Chapter 2

1 König, Karl, *Der innere Pfad,* p. 45f. Trans. by Ireine Czech.

2 With regard to the path that König took in relationship to Rudolf Steiner compare Hans Müller-Wiedemann's finely perceptive descriptions. '[König] lived and stood for this pupilship as a free relationship in a dialogue which was constantly being renewed' (HMW, p. 47).

The available diary entries show, amongst other things, how intensively König occupied himself, not only with Rudolf Steiner's lectures and writings, but also with Steiner's life. (Feb 23, 1955: 'Strongly sense the coming of February 27, and begin to read the autobiography in the evening.' Feb 25, 1955: 'I have immersed myself in the life of the landscape and this wonderful child. It is as if I am reading this book for the first time.' Feb 27, 1955: 'The night was peaceful and good. In the morning we have glorious weather, filled with sun, snow and clarity. Rudolf Steiner was born 94 years ago today. I read the autobiography with an even deeper joy and try to accompany the friends at the Offering Service.' March 13, 1955: 'The night was reasonable; in the morning read the last two chapters of the autobiography. The extraordinary miracles of this life-book have accompanied me the past weeks, and I am thankful that I may carry it in myself in such a lively and strong way.')

From the very beginning, König's closest colleagues were aware of his inner connection to Rudolf Steiner in that 'working with Karl König meant working with Rudolf Steiner.' Anke Weihs continued, 'König regularly studied Rudolf Steiner's basic writings with us, as well as his lectures, and led us step by step into a new world in which he himself moved freely, creatively, courageously and in a future-orientated way, unfailingly preserving the original integrity of Rudolf Steiner's spiritual science. Thus his reverence for his teacher became a lesson for us...' (HMW, p. 152).

The remaining diary entries are incomplete and fragmentary in nature and as such do not allow more precise documentation of the course of development of Karl König's relationship to Rudolf Steiner — that is to say, of König's ever-transforming encounter with the 'spiritual countenance' of Rudolf Steiner. Both Hans-Heinrich Engel and Hans Müller-Wiedemann with whom König had very close relationships, have indicated that Karl König's connection to Rudolf Steiner deepened once again during the last years of his life. 'It also became apparent that the connection to his teacher Rudolf Steiner had become still more intimate during those last years.' (Hans-Heinrich Engel, quoted in HMW, p. 291); 'Ever closer did Rudolf Steiner's spirit form come to him; ever more open did his own life become to the intention of his teacher' (HMW, p. 439).

On March 30, 1960, six years before his own death, Karl König concluded his memorial address for the thirtieth anniversary of Rudolf Steiner's death with the following words:

Dear friends, that in 1960 groups of people still may speak about the spiritual essence of the human being, that they are truly capable of connecting the spiritual in the human being with the hierarchical beings, with Angels, Archangels, Archai, Exousiai, with Dynameis and Kyriotetes, with Thrones and Seraphim and Cherubim, and to know that we exist in their memory, in their being, in their activity; that their world is not separate from ours but inside us, with us and around us: this is only possible through Rudolf Steiner. And there is not much difference whether five or five thousand, twelve or forty-eight still consciously carry this truth within themselves. The balance [to the Ahrimanic subnature] is a given. And therefore the earth and development in the name of Christ is ensured.' (Karl König Archive, Camphill).

In connection to the foregoing it is also important to realize that Karl König understood the laying of the Foundation Stone by Rudolf Steiner at the Christmas Conference as the fundamental 'renewal of the human image' and as such was the esoteric basis of all of König's curative education work.

3 Rudolf Steiner, *Anthroposophical Leading Thoughts*, p. 60.
4 Rudolf Steiner, *Karmic Relationships*, Vol. 7, p. 115.
5 Rudolf Steiner, *Karmic Relationships*, Vol. 7, p. 115. Karl König certainly must have sought reference to Steiner with regard to his frequently poor condition in the morning and the agonizing headaches that often forced him to stay in bed for hours, ('In the morning I still stay in bed and rest. It is my head again and the pain is dreadful. I become aware of all my incompetencies and how little I am able to control my body.' July 14, 1954.). In this sense, König must have understood this not only as an expression of a difficult return to an earthly physical body, but equally on the basis of destiny-karmic considerations. Rudolf Steiner, in his Breslau lecture of June 14, 1924, said the following in this regard:

> A very burdensome karma, a karma that is difficult to bear, radiates unhealthy material deposits into the head, whereas a good karma radiates health-bringing deposits. And it is here that the spiritual and the natural make contact. The good in a man's karma radiates the healthy states of the organism into the head in the morning and carifies it; healthy elements radiate upwards from good karma. From bad karma, from the rresidue of whatever guilt has been incurred, unhealthy deposits in the human orgnism are reduced to a kind of vapour which rises up in the head. The head then feels dull and heavy. The weaving of karma right into the physical can be perceived from the condition prevailing on waking in the morning. (*Karmic Relationships*, Vol. 7, pp. 115f.)

6 With regard to this subject see also König's later commentary *Geschichte und Schicksal des jüdischen Volkes*, as well as Hans Müller-Wiedemann's '1965 und das jüdische Schicksal,' in HMW, pp. 407–29.
7 Compare HMW, pp. 128ff.
8 Compare Peter Selg: *Mysterium Cordis.*

Chapter 3

1 On the Comburg, three days before a lecture to anthroposophical doctors on the subject of the cardiovascular system, König noted: 'I review the details of ontogenesis, of the blood vessels, and realize that while the vitelline sac circulation is a recapitulation of the Tree of Life, the placenta circulation is the image of the Tree of Knowledge. Instead of the Tree of Life, the human being receives the heart because it carries both death *and* life in it. Also studied the early stages of development of the physical body and discover completely astonishing correspondences. Try to order it all, to express it, but the power to formulate is missing and I must hope that it will come in the time before the lec-

ture. In any case, the material has come together.' (April 24, 1965)

2 Compare the outstanding edition of these lectures by Hans Müller-Wiedemann and Klaus Dumke, *Karl König: Auferweckung und Auferstehung.*

3 Following an Epiphany lecture at Camphill in 1953, Karl König made the following notes: 'When I ... entered the Hall, it was more like the atmosphere of a cinema, and it was difficult to speak. All that I wanted to say remained with me, as if behind a curtain, and no creative work was possible. Depressing to experience such a demonstration of one's own inadequacy.' Four weeks later following a London lecture: 'Three hundred people come to hear me, but it is difficult to speak. Only towards the middle of the lecture do I become a little warmed through and am able to touch hearts. Nevertheless it was not a good lecture; it had no structure and there was too much talk.' (Feb 2, 1953).

4 'During the lectures I thought I sensed how the devotion to the imaginative element and the surprises that arose swept him away at times.' (Erhard Fucke, p. 86).

5 In his lecture cycle, *Die Evolution vom Gesichtspunkt des Wahrhaftigen,* on Oct 31, 1911 Rudolf Steiner emphasized the significance and necessity of 'fantasy-like imaginations' and indicated how essential it would be for this faculty to be developed in the future. Within the context of an examination of the relational structure of higher hierarchical beings, Rudolf Steiner brought a great image at the end of his lecture presentation, recommending that it should be developed further, saying the following:

> What we have to achieve is the metamorphosis of the impressions we receive into fantasy-like imaginations. Even if the images are clumsy, if they are anthropomorphic, or if these hierarchical beings look like winged people, that is unimportant. The missing element will be given to us, and the extraneous matter will be discarded. If we just live into these imags, then we do something which will lead us to these beings. (pp. 20f).

There appears to be some significance to Karl König's absolute engagement of will concerning Steiner's recommendations in the above-described context; therefore, rather than underestimating or overestimating König's individual descriptions, it is possible to see their meaning within a prospective schooling process.

6 'In a conversation with the author shortly before his death, König referred to the preparing of lectures as the most cherished times of his life.' (HMW, p. 320).

7 In this connection Rudolf Steiner said (in *Die Verbindung zwischen Lebenden und Toten,* p. 214):

> Much would be gained if ... those living would connect with those who have died and would try to maintain the continuity

of evolution more consciously. Whether it is a freely chosen relationship or one that is a result of a karmic connection, the support of those sending the rays of their working from the spiritual world, is something of immensely significance, if we live consciously with it.

8 Carlo Pietzner, who was present at the lecture, wrote the following about König's visit to the USA: 'This last lecture was like a celebration, and the one who officiated spoke in the living presence of Rudolf Steiner himself.' (HMW, p. 346). Karl König also experienced 'Rudolf Steiner's living presence' in strongly tangible ways outside of his lectures: One year before his death he noted the following with regard to a profound encounter with a spiritual being that occurred before an important conversation with the Executive Council in Dornach: 'As I sit with Georg [von Arnim] and Alix [Roth] at breakfast in the hotel and we discuss the coming meeting, I suddenly experience Rudolf Steiner's presence. This presence brings tears of surprise to my eyes and I greet him with the words of the Michael Meditation. He nods his head at me. Now I have been anointed for the conversation.' (March 29, 1965).

9 Karl König, 'Die Substanz Sepia' later published in *Beiträge zu einer Erweiterung der Heilkunst*. Compare my study 'Erinnerung an Dr Karl König und seine medizinischen Aufsätze' (Issue 4, pp. 228f).

10 König's essay 'Die Schicksale Sigmund Freuds. Zu seinem 100. Geburtstag am 6. Mai 1956' appeared soon after in *Die Drei*.

11 On the publication of the plays Peter Roth wrote in his foreword:

The plays occupy a special place in Karl König's creative life. They were not written as 'works of art,' as parts of an ivory tower art; they were written when a special constellation of the social organism within which he lived inspired him — a constellation of people, of events in this social organism, of the festival being of the time of year relating to this organism, and so on. It is the purpose of any art, and especially so in our time, to lift the Special into the General; to show the validity of concrete situations.

In retrospect, the fruitfulness of this kind of play writing was due, as far as one can divine, to two inter-related aspects of Karl König's being. The one was that the spring-mood of his soul, a continuously budding creative hopefulness, was unthinkable without its striving to become 'word'; in lectures and articles, in talks, poems and plays. The 'sprouting' quality of their words is very impressive. The other aspect, which is especially relevant to the plays, was his extraordinary longing and devotion towards Christianity. He had great knowledge of the various aspects of the world, and he permeated this knowledge with the light of the insights and understanding of Anthroposophy. That *Anthroposophia* wishes to share and enlighten the destiny of Christianity: this conviction was the main foundation and aim of his life. The Mystery of Golgotha took place in Spring: Karl König's plays in their manifoldness are a manifestation of this fact. (p.5).

See HMW, pp. 321ff for a specifically spiritual-scientific characterization of Karl König's plays and also the noteworthy performances.

Chapter 4

1 Compare HMW, particularly pp. 191ff. and pp. 219ff.

2 Compare HMW, pp. 81ff.

3 Compare Rudolf Steiner, *Mysterienstätten des Mittelalters,* pp. 159ff. (published in English as *The Easter Festival in the Evolution of the Mysteries,* lecture of April 22, 1924.)

4 According to Hans Müller-Wiedemann, Karl König introduced her 'most intimate name' in his internal address at the opening of Camphill Hall on Sep 20, 1962 'in the context of a comprehensive esoteric history in connection with the sacrifice of Iphigenia, through which Irish Christianity was in former times able to ensoul and illumine the etheric landscape of Europe.' p. 540.

Using a long letter of statement by Karl König as reference, Hans Müller-Wiedemann continued in this regard:

The sacrifice of Iphigenia, which is an archetypal picture of a consciously grasped spiritual task whence healing can flow for the transformation of the lower, unpurified life of soul, had what could be described as an 'external' aspect that was inscribed in the daily sacrificial service of those who built up Camphill through the work of their hands. As this archetypal image — which in a remarkable way remained true to the Community through all its transformations, in that it was kept alive by human individuals — became more inward, it found expression in the name of the Hall. The individual sacrifices which the self voluntarily makes when it receives the aims of humanity into its life are a condition for all community building. Spirit-recollection is the prerequisite for harnessing the will to service on this path.

In a personal letter dated December 16, 1960 to South Africa, probably referring to the building of the Hall, König wrote:

Iphigenia is not abundance but poverty. She prepares the table on which the sacrament can be fulfilled. That is why she moved to the Black Sea, to dark Scythia, because there she had to prepare the teachings of the Buddha and his mystery centre. By that time Iphigenia had already outgrown the service of

Artemis and — as priestess of the Moon — had risen to become the servant of Mercury. As a result her family disintegrates; the son becomes his mother's murderer. Iphigenia's sacrifice prepares a new world to be established: through the destruction of Troy not only can Greece emerge but also Buddha can take up his mission. Thus the Black Sea is the mother of 'inner Europe'; there is prepared what unfolds later. (HMW, p. 348).

For Rudolf Steiner's description of the Colchis Mysteries of the Black Sea and the initiation of the Franz of Assisi individuality in the mysteries of moral 'healing love' through the Buddha and Christ impulses see Rudolf Steiner's *The Spiritual Foundation of Morality*, as well as HMW, p. 114. Hans Müller-Wiedemann's assumption that Karl König's letter about Iphigenia had a direct connection with the Hall building is unlikely considering the night experience described by König in his diary on June 18, 1962, i.e. eighteen months *after* the letter was written.

5 On April 16, 1944 Karl König noted in his diary: 'In the morning the Risen One appears at the altar. The back of His hands are laid on the altar, His countenance of light is hidden behind the picture. He radiates undreamt-of goodness. If I close my eyes I cannot see, but can sense Him. I am so deeply moved by this that I can hardly speak. He disappears after the reading of the Gospel.'

On the other hand, on June 21, 1953 he wrote: 'Again and again it is so moving to experience the children as so embedded in spiritual substance.'

6 Compare HMW, pp. 182ff and 455ff.

7 Karl König (1953), quoted in HMW, p. 167.

8 In HMW, p. 186.

9 Rudolf Steiner, *Aus der Akasha-Chronik. Das Fünfte Evangelium*, pp. 207f. Following a renewed Whitsun reading of the second Christiana lecture, Karl König noted on May 29, 1955: 'Am deeply moved by the description of the apostles before Whitsun. For me it is as if a kind of memory picture of the forty days also lights up in my soul.' (May 29, 1955).

10 See my books, *Rudolf Steiner und das Fünfte Evangelium* and *Die Kultur der Selbstlosigkeit*.

11 Karl König wrote the following with regard to the reality of the Christ-encounter within the religious services: 'These services have become an essential part of the Movement, as we have experienced the deep and lasting healing power which they have instilled in the children. For their souls long for real religious content, and the take it in with reverence every Sunday.' (HMW, p.183).

12 Quoted in HMW, p.459. See also Note 14 below.

13 'A bleak Bible Evening about the sick at the pool of Bethesda. It is nev-

ertheless moving to experience *the immediate power of the Good* in the Bible Evening.' (Feb 14, 1953, emphasis added). On October 6, 1965, just six months before his death, Karl König wrote about the necessary 'renewal' and future form of the Bible Evening:

The transformation of the Bible Evening from a traditional, Gabrielic form into one that is new and Michaelic has only partly come about. From now on, whatever Gabrielic robes still clothe the Bible Evening must be shed. The Bible Evening must be set free and find its way forward and onward from the initial traditional mould that was necessary to begin with.

The following indicate the way forward: Firstly, waiting in silence and the introductory verse stand under the sign of the Rose Cross. Everything radiates from there.

Secondly, the common meal in whatever form, and the conversation during the meal may be called an act of 'the celebration of community.' This is where a vessel should be built up that becomes the receptacle for the event in the following part.

Thirdly, because the Word of Christ is revealed in the Gospel reading and in the conversation that follows it becomes the radiating content of the community-vessel that had been built up before. A Grail Act must be accomplished here.

Fourthly, in conclusion a word must be spoken that is concerned with the seeing of the Christ in the etheric. For what was prepared through the work of the Rosicrucians comes to fulfilment in the Second Coming, the re-appearance of the Christ in the etheric realm of the earthly world.

If the Bible Evening could be renewed in this way, then it will be raised up into the Light of Michael.' (Karl König Archive, Camphill).

14 One year previously, on the Saturday night before Palm Sunday, König wrote the following about the latter part of the day and the Bible Evening: 'There are many conversations in the afternoon and it is possible to sort out some things amongst people. Then the eve of Palm Sunday clearly comes up before me. It is as if a curtain within my innermost soul has been opened and a quiet sense of the substance of Holy Week presents itself. I experience 'thinking' as a donkey that must now be picked up by the two apostles, the memory and conscience relating to its own existence, in order to become carriers of the gently stirring Easter Light.

All this lives in me, but is completely shattered by the terrible gaping emptiness of the Bible Evening at Newton Dee. The friends arrive unprepared, gloomy and sleepy, and nothing transforms into devotion and gratitude. I come back to Camphill, despairing and deeply ashamed. Is this the result of all the years?' (March 28, 1953).

15 In HMW, p. 295.

16 Ten months previously, on May 19, 1953, König had noted: 'These encounters are an important part of what I am doing here, because people trust me, in conversation they are able to see themselves as if in a mirror and can raise themselves above themselves.' Hans Müller-Wiedemann on the other hand described the particular conversational atmosphere with Karl König as follows:

A kind of fullness of being was evident whenever he spoke or listened attentively, and it was perhaps largely through this perception that one felt oneself to be wholly accepted as a partner in conversation, in that through feeling free to speak one had been granted the opportunity to put all superficialities aside. König had a highly developed sense for what was essential in a person, and this sense also enabled him to discover the potential which as yet lay slumbering. He could comfort, not always only through advice or explanations but through his capacity to radiate something which became apparent in the folds of his countenance and his eyes, and which evoked a more elevated quality than is usual among human beings. When sitting opposite him in conversation, one had the impression of extreme concentration, together with a wholly open mood of expectancy, as though one were his first — and sole — conversation partner. One noticed that he was prepared, and I doubt that he ever conducted a conversation in private without due inner preparation.' (HMW, p. 313).

17 Compare HMW, p. 200.

18 Karl König also applied this methodical scrutiny to the form of anthroposophical study. On January 4, 1956 he noted in his diary: 'Together with the friends at Camphill in the evening, read the last lecture of the *Fifth Gospel* to them. Sense very clearly that this way of reading is no longer valid. The aura that otherwise surrounded the Doctor's words has been lost, because thirty years have passed, and we will have to learn to find each other in a completely new way. But how?'

Chapter 5

1 Karl König, 'Autobiographical Fragment' in König and Selg, *Karl König: My Task*, p. 28

2 'I have always sense that what wants to come about at Lake Constance must be understood against the background of Ephesus ... There is a strong destiny pointing to the individuality of Ita Wegman, and we must try to raise it into consciousness more and more.' (From a letter written by Karl König to Erika von Arnim, June 29, 1964).

3 Karl König spoke and wrote repeatedly about the very real help that the

Camphill community, and indeed the whole of human civilization receives through the handicapped children. Ten months before he left earthly life, König wrote the following to the parents connected to the Camphill School and the village community at Lake Constance:

We should all be increasingly filled with the idea that these children are our teachers; teachers in a higher sense. For they have taken their destiny — to be bent and deformed, ill-prepared for life and retarded — upon themselves. They do not complain and are not surly. They also do not accuse or bewail their fate. Rather do they take their being different courageously upon themselves, in the way that a person carries his cross on his shoulders, and say 'yes' to it unreservedly.

We should not think that they do not understand who and how they are. They know this very well and nevertheless remain courageous, cheerful and full of hope. Should we not follow their example? All of us? Which of us does not let our courage fail and lose our hope more often than our children? It is in this sense that I mean they are our teachers. But also in another sense. Each of our children contributes to the winning of a great battle which has been fought by people for thousands of years. The whole of history, in all its suffering, deeds and achievements, is an expression of this battle. It is the ongoing battle that the spirit wages against the needs of the body. That body which since the Fall has been ensnared and penetrated by our soul. The spirit of each person's individuality lighting up in his soul tries ever and again to free itself from the grip of sin. If the body is healthy, we succumb all too easily to its drives, desires and longings. But if it is ailing and infirm, it reminds us of the hardships and troubles of existence.

That is what our children constantly bring home to us. They show us the other side of life, which is just as necessary and important as that in which we are immersed every day. Here too our children are our teachers. They help us — through their daily appearance, through their hardships and tribulations — to keep the spiritual spark of our souls awake and not to forget the oil in our lamps. Our children are not warriors but gentle, though constant, admonishers in the great battle of the history of mankind.

What would we do without them? Would not the whole of humanity lose its social balance if sorrow and pain, differentness and specialness were not to appear constantly before us? Only superficial people could be of the opinion that the world should be without sickness and need. If this were so, how would we know what joy and the sense of gladness is? Is not the love that rules over everything both pain and joy? Is not grace both challenge and conquest? Is not faith both doubt and blessedness?

In such moments we want to remember this; we want to say a full, unreserved 'yes' to our children and to their and our destiny, to this difficult task. Only this 'yes' gives our children the true foundation on which they can stand and live. Only such a 'yes' gives them the solidity of their and our existence. For only then do we reaffirm the words which Christ spoke to his disciples, that those alone are blessed who are sorrowful. They shall be comforted, but being comforted they will give still greater comfort. (HMW, pp. 476f.)

With regard to Kaspar Hauser as — according to König — 'patron saint' of handicapped children and 'he who preserves the 'image of God' compare Karl König, 'Die Geschichte von Kaspar Hauser,' and *Auch eine Weihnachtsgeschichte,* as well as HMW, pp. 205ff ('Ita Wegman's death. Kaspar's Arrival').

4 See also my Michaelic study *Friedrich Schiller.*

5 Compare my study, dedicated to Karl König and Karl Schubert, *Der therapeutische Blick.*

6 Steiner, *The Mystery of the Wound,* lecture of Aug 14, 1914.

Bibliography

Fucke, Erhard, *Siebzehn Begegnungen,* Stuttgart 1996.

König, Karl, *Auch eine Weihnachtsgeschichte,* Stuttgart 1998.

—, *Ewige Kindheit,* (lectures, Vienna, Oct 18–16, 1964) manuscript print, n.d.

—, *Geschichte und Schicksal des jüdischen Volkes,* manuscript print, n.d.

—, 'Die Geschichte von Kaspar Hauser,' in *Die Brücke. Mitteilungen aus dem Freundeskreis Camphill,* 1987

—, *Der innere Pfad. Sieben Vorträge über Meditation und geistige Schulung,* Stuttgart 1995.

—, *Plays for Christmas,* Camphill Press 1981.

—, 'Die Schicksale Sigmund Freuds. Zu seinem 100. Geburtstag am 6. Mai 1956,' in *Die Drei,* Nos. 4 & 5, 1956.

—, 'Die Substanz Sepia,' in *Beiträge zu einer Erweiterung der Heilkunst nach geistesswisenschaftlichen Geischtspunkten,* Vol.8, No. 7/8, 1955.

König, Karl, and Selg, Peter, *Karl König: My Task,* Edinburgh 2008.

Müller-Wiedemann, Hans, *Karl König, a Central European Biography of the Twentieth Century.*

Müller-Wiedemann, Hans and Dumke, Klaus, *Karl König: Auferweckung und Auferstehung* (four lectures, Easter 1965 in Föhrenbühl), Stuttgart 1997.

Selg, Peter, 'Erinnerung an Dr Karl König und seine medizinischen Aufsätze in den "Beiträgen zu einer Erweiterung der Heilkunst" (1950-1966),' in *Der Merkurstab,* Vol. 53, Issue 2-4, 2000.

—, *Friedrich Schiller. Die Geistigkeit des Willens,* Dornach 2005.

—, *Die Kultur der Selbstlosigkeit,* Dornach 2006.

—, *Mysterium Cordis. Studien zur sakramentalen Physiologie des Herzorgans,* Dornach 2003.

—, *Rudolf Steiner und das Fünfte Evangelium,* Dornach 2005.

—, *Der therapeutische Blick. Rudolf Steiner sieht Kinder,* Dornach 2005.

Steiner, Rudolf, *Anthroposophische Leitsätze,* (Gesamtausgabe (GA) 26) Dornach 1989. English: *Anthroposophical Leading Thoughts,* London 1973.

—, *Aus der Akasha-Chronik. Das Fünfte Evangelium,* (GA 148) Dornach 1992. English: *The Fifth Gospel, from the Akashik Record,* Forest Row 1998.

—, *Esoterische Betrachtungen karmischer Zusammenhänge,* Vol. 5, (GA 239) Dornach 1985. English: Karmic Relationships, Vol 7, London 1973.

—, *Die Evolution vom Gesichtspunkt des Wahrhaftigen,* (GA 132) Dornach 1999. English: *Inner Experience of Evolution,* Massachussets 2008.

—, *Inneres Wesen des Menschen,* [Norrköping lecture of May 29, 1912] (GA 153) Dornach 1978. English: *The Spiritual Foundations of Morality,* New York 1995.

—, *Mysterienstätten des Mittelalters, Rosenkreutzertum und modernes Einweihungsprinzip,* (GA 233a) Dornach 1991. English lecture of April 22, 1924: *The Easter Festival in the Evolution of the Mysteries,* New York 1988.

—, *Die Verbindung zwischen Lebenden und Toten,* (GA 168) Dornach 1995.

—, lecture of Aug 14, 1914 in *Beiträge zur Rudolf Steiner Gesamtausgabe,* No. 108. English: *The Mystery of the Wound,* manuscript, Camphill Libary.

Index

Karl König's collected works are being published in English by Floris Books, Edinburgh and in German by Verlag Freies Geistesleben, Stuttgart. They are issued by the Karl König Archive, Aberdeen in co-operation with the Ita Wegman Institute for Basic Research into Anthroposophy, Arlesheim. They seek to encompass the entire, wide-ranging literary estate of Karl König, including his books, essays, manuscripts, lectures, diaries, notebooks, his extensive correspondence and his artistic works. The publications will fall into twelve subjects. The aim is to open up König's work in a systematic way and make it accessible. This work is supported by many people in different countries.

Overview of Karl König Archive subjects

Medicine and study of the human being
Curative education and social therapy
Psychology and education
Agriculture and science
Social questions
The Camphill movement
Christianity and the festivals
Anthroposophy
Spiritual development
History and biographies
Artistic and literary works
Karl König's biography

Karl König Archive
Camphill House
Milltimber
Aberdeen AB13 0AN
United Kingdom
www.karl-koenig-archive.net
kk.archive@camphill.net

Ita Wegman Institute for Basic
Research into Anthroposophy
Pfeffingerweg 1a
4144 Arlesheim
Switzerland
www.wegmaninstitut.ch
koenigarchiv@wegmaninstitut.ch